"*Awaken Your Financial STAR* unpacks confusion and brings clarity to the complexities of finance and investment in today's challenging and often contentious economic environment. It is a field manual for overcoming inertia, ignorance, and the limiting beliefs that hold people back from financial success which awaits them. The principles here are timeless in their wisdom and strikingly modern in their application. I recommend this book to anyone ready to turn intention into action and reclaim control over their financial future."

—MARK MacCARLEY,
Managing Attorney, MacCarley & Rosen, PLC

"I am captivated . . . I feel today it is more urgent than ever to become stable in our own ability to live a good life . . . It's beautifully inspiring and a clear example of the power of persistence."

—S. LEE WRIGHT, CEO,
Conscious Design with S. Lee Wright

"*Awaken Your Financial STAR* comes across as a combination motivational and personal finance book. Sometimes you need the motivational part to get started in life."

—KENT WOO, CFA

EDWARD M. BRADY, CFA

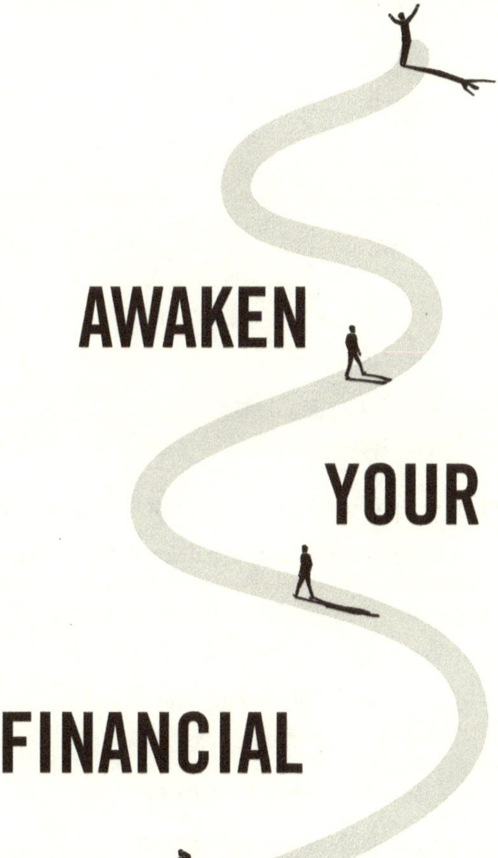

AWAKEN YOUR FINANCIAL STAR

A FIELD MANUAL FOR BUILDING REAL WEALTH IN AN UNCERTAIN WORLD

Cover and interior design by David Ter-Avanesyan/Ter33Design LLC

Cover image by Shutterstock.com

Paperback ISBN: 979-8-9957305-4-5

Hardcover ISBN: 979-8-9957305-5-2

E-Book ISBN: 979-8-9957305-6-9

CONTENTS

DISCLAIMER

The information provided by Edward Brady is for *educational and informational purposes only*, and the information contained herein is not intended as a specific recommendation for any security or real estate. Examples are purely for illustration purposes. It should not be considered financial, investment, legal, or tax advice. Edward Brady is not a lawyer, a licensed financial advisor, an investment advisor, a broker-dealer, or a tax professional.

Although Edward Brady is a real estate broker (California DRE# 01066142), all strategies, examples, and opinions expressed are *general in nature*. They are not tailored to any individual's unique circumstances. Before making any financial decisions, you should consult with a qualified professional who understands your personal situation, goals, and risk tolerance.

Investing and financial planning involve risk, including the possible loss of principal. Past performance is not indicative of future results. No guarantees are made regarding the accuracy, completeness, or reliability of the information presented, nor of any specific outcome or financial result.

By using this content, you acknowledge and agree that Edward Brady shall not be held liable for any direct, indirect, incidental, or consequential damages resulting from the use or misuse of the information provided. You are solely responsible for your financial decisions.

The views expressed are Edward Brady's alone. The institutions below have not endorsed this book, including eXp Realty, Inc., Chartered Financial Analyst (CFA) Institute, Financial Industry Regulatory Authority (FINRA), FINRA Institute, Association of Certified Fraud Examiners (ACFE), or the Securities and Exchange Commission (SEC). Therefore, this book reflects Edward Brady's views and may not necessarily reflect those of the above institutions' leadership, management, or staff.

PREFACE

Dear reader,

This book is for you, and for all the wonderful souls who have guided, supported, and inspired me along the way. Thank you for opening these pages and allowing me to share this journey with you. I hope that these words help you discover new freedom and possibilities through investing. If this book brings you value or a spark of hope, I'd be grateful if you could recommend it to someone who might benefit, so we can help even more people find their paths forward.

With gratitude, I will donate a portion of the net profits from this book to the 100 Billion Meals Challenge[1].

Thank you to the many people and institutions that helped me learn and grow: the Chartered Financial Analyst (CFA) Institute, my former Securities and Exchange Commission (SEC) colleagues, the Financial Industry Regulatory Authority (FINRA) Institute, and the Association of Certified Fraud Examiners (ACFE).

To every soul who wears or wore a uniform, your sacrifices will never be without meaning, whether witnessed by thousands or known only to God. The values you carry define you. To live by a code is a rare and sacred privilege, even in those moments when it costs you dearly; perhaps especially then. To abandon those values is a quieter kind of death. May God grant you a long life, rich with stories of the moments when you held the line, even when it was hard. This book is my heartfelt offering of gratitude. Thank you.

1. *100 Billion Meals*, https://www.100billionmeals.org/.

To my wonderful wife, your unwavering support, love, and encouragement have been my guiding star. Your laughter and kindness bring joy to my days, and your strength inspires me. Traveling the world with you has been a great adventure.

Thank you to the authors listed in the Further Reading section, whose wisdom, shared in speeches and books, has inspired me over the years. "The ultimate human freedom is the power to choose, to respond, to change."[2]

Like those who came before us, let us live with dignity, pursuing freedom, possibilities, and happiness, whether for a moment or a lifetime.

Steadfast,

Ed

---

2. Stephen Covey, *The Seven Habits of Highly Effective People* (2003).

INTRODUCTION

A journey of a thousand miles begins with a single step.
—Lao Tzu

Namaste.

In ancient Sanskrit, "namaste" means "I see the light in you." Whether you feel it yet or not, something in you is ready to rise. That may be why you picked up this book.

You might wonder why a personal finance book begins with a greeting like this. But money is not just numbers on a spreadsheet. Wealth shapes your confidence, your choices, your stress, your freedom, and your life. Your financial life is deeply personal.

Why Start with Spirituality?

Most of us were not taught about money. We were taught how to work hard, be grateful, and be "good," but not how to build freedom. Wealth and power may expose our weaknesses, and many of us (including me) absorbed the idea that wanting those things made us selfish and shallow. I grew up hearing that money corrupted people. Perhaps you felt the same tension: desire mixed with fear of what money might do to you. However, not having money is not a virtue; it is a vulnerability. Whether rich or poor, we are responsible for our actions. Money *amplifies our capabilities.*

Marcus Aurelius, a Roman Emperor, demonstrated that wealth and power are not inherently corrupt; rather, they reveal a person's character. There are many examples of good character among the very wealthy, including George Washington, Andrew Carnegie, Mahatma Gandhi, Nelson Mandela, Bill Gates, and Warren Buffett.

Currency is neither good nor bad; it is a tool. It can buy you toys, travel, time, options, safety, and the life you want. Once I realized that money is just a tool, I stopped blaming money for human behavior.

Now, with living expenses rising faster than salaries, it is necessary to have financial clarity, and it is more than just a matter of survival. True wealth is not just a number. It is more than just having confidence in paying your bills without distress. It's being able to breathe. It's having choices.

To me, true wealth is being unburdened. Two people with the same net worth may have totally different life experiences: One may be enslaved to the toys they have accumulated, and the other may be free to live with purpose. That is what this book teaches.

My goal is to help you awaken the financial STAR within you. Whether you believe it yet or not, you are capable of building stability, confidence, and a future that feels unrestricted. Whether you are starting your career, rebuilding after setbacks, or just feeling uneasy about your finances, this journey is for you.

Early Lessons: From Chaos to Clarity

My journey began in a chaotic household where I struggled in school and doubted myself. Through navigating setbacks, working hard, and being guided by mentors, I learned that financial freedom is possible for anyone, including you. In these pages, you'll discover how to turn setbacks into lessons, build lasting wealth, and find peace beyond numbers.

Let me start by introducing myself and sharing the stories of my early struggles to highlight the moments that eventually awakened me to the true nature of wealth. Perhaps you may learn something valuable from my struggles, without having to repeat them yourself.

My large Irish Catholic family included three boys and three girls. We were like the Brady bunch, but we were the "unsupervised mediator required" version. Our house was chaotic. Once, the yelling was so loud that my neighbor asked if I needed a place to live for a while. I did not grow up wealthy or in the ideal household. My father struggled with anger, but my siblings made up for my father's shortcomings, and I always felt loved. My brothers were excellent role models, but my unstable home made it very hard for me to pay attention in school. I daydreamed when I should have been paying attention, so I earned poor grades in grammar school and high school, which led me to think I was dumb. Despite my upbringing, I achieved financial freedom, and you can too, no matter where you started from.

Finding Purpose Beyond Myself

My Catholic upbringing taught me to live life according to the spirit of the law, so conscience became my guiding star. Growing up in Westchester, a middle-class suburb of Los Angeles (LA), California, I became aware of wealth disparity from a pretty early age. In high school, I volunteered to help feed people who were experiencing homelessness at the Los Angeles Mission soup kitchen as part of a class assignment. That experience helped me to recognize the value in helping others. Over the years, I've found that having a purpose beyond myself is rewarding.

A good-paying summer internship came up for the LA Department of Water and Power (DWP). I remember someone saying, "You will never get that job." I figured they were right, but I really wanted the job because it paid well, so I tried anyway. For the DWP summer internship, I worked as a laborer, clearing fire hazards and digging ditches. It was good, hard work, and I made friends. At the end of each day, I was tired and dirty but felt good. I also got a glimpse of the enormous mansions in Bel Air, one of LA's wealthiest neighborhoods. Seeing what was possible inspired me, and envy fueled my desire. Eventually, I realized that if I gave in to envy and compared myself to others, I would never be satisfied. However, I also learned that wealth would enable me to live well and to help others.

Inspiration from Family and Mentors

My mother proudly told stories about how my jovial grandfather (Pop Pops) had doubled his money in the stock market after selling his successful cost consulting business. I admired Pop Pops. He was a US Army Reserve officer who served on active duty during World War II and later authored several books after his retirement. I remember the joy I felt when visiting my grandparents, and I would have enjoyed learning about finance from Pop Pops and getting to know him better. Unfortunately, Pop Pops passed away before I became interested in investing.

Although Pop Pops inspired me by his example, anyone could learn the way I did by reading hundreds of self-help and investing books. Those authors became my mentors, so I have included the absolute best of their books in the Further Reading section for your future reference.

Building Skills and Overcoming Self-Doubt

At nineteen years old, I obtained my real estate license while attending school full-time, and I started selling real estate and working a second job to pay the bills. In 1991, California experienced a housing slump, so I quit selling real estate and refocused my efforts on school. The work ethic I learned in real estate enabled me to earn nearly straight A's, and I let go of the destructive belief that I was dumb and replaced it with a belief in myself as a hard worker. Maintaining a positive self-image is critical as your perception of yourself may hinder or accelerate your success. My passion for investing led me to study finance in college, and I graduated with honors, earning a degree in finance with a minor in real estate.

Early Success and Lessons

During college, I learned about mental discipline, stock investing, and the value of diversification. William J. O'Neal spoke at my university. Mr. O'Neal was a famous, successful investor who authored the book *How to Make Money in*

Stocks and founded Investor's Business Daily (IBD). After Mr. O'Neal's speech, I spoke briefly with him, and he encouraged me to continue my path in finance. I traded stocks with the bit of money I had saved and made my initial investment many times over. After about two years of successful trading, I projected that at that rate of return, I would be a multimillionaire before age thirty.

One day, I incorrectly anticipated a stock move and lost about 20 percent of my portfolio in a few hours because I had put everything into a single stock. I'd overestimated my appetite for risk and discounted the benefits of diversification. One of the benefits of diversification is that it protects your self-confidence and preserves your courage and appetite for risk.

Real Estate Tax Benefits

My former landlords, a couple in their fifties, also inspired me as they purchased thirty properties in LA over the years. With their casual attire and modest demeanor, few people knew they were very wealthy. I learned that my landlords withdrew thirty million dollars tax-free from their rental properties and reinvested it without incurring any tax liability because loans are not taxable. My landlords borrowed less than their rental properties supported. Afterward, interest rates fell, inflation continued, and real estate appreciated. My landlords taught me the unparalleled tax benefits of buying real estate.

Staying True to Your Values

After college, I interviewed with stock brokerage firms that promoted aggressive sales tactics. One retail broker, for example, recommended only equities it bought and sold for its own account while charging an undisclosed markup fee; it was a dishonest practice that raised apparent conflicts of interest. I declined that job because I felt the practice was unethical; more importantly, I followed my conscience rather than chasing money. If you follow the principles in this book, the money will come, so be true to yourself, enjoy the journey, and you will live a life you can someday look back at with pride.

You Are Either Winning or Learning

During my late twenties, I learned many things.

I invested money and time in a multilevel marketing business and lost everything, then stubbornly kept opening credit cards, using one to pay for another. I found myself with no revenue, unemployed, and with a tremendous amount of credit card debt. Even though I knew what I was doing wasn't working, I felt paralyzed and failed to change course. The lesson was twofold: Cash flow is life-giving for businesses, and learning to pivot is an essential skill for entrepreneurs.

It can seem overwhelming when you accumulate too much debt and cannot figure out how you are going to eat, or pay utilities and rent, let alone become financially free. I remember living in my small, dark apartment in Glendale, California. I felt sorry for myself and was lonely, and I was living on peanut-butter-and-jelly sandwiches. I could not pay my bills without using my credit cards. At age twenty-seven, I was broke; worse, I had a massive amount of credit card debt and no income. Yes, I had a negative net worth; however, I felt paralyzed by my pessimistic mindset, so I eventually learned the importance of attitude.

Next, I worked as a limo driver for a while. One day, I was driving a friendly, wealthy, well-dressed man. I still distinctly remember the conversation I overheard between the man and his wife on the speakerphone. The man told his wife, "Honey, we made $100 million today selling the company." The wife replied, without a hint of excitement in her voice, "That's nice. Can you bring home some milk?" As we pulled into the grocery store, I thought, "He seems like a regular guy; maybe I can still be successful too." So I learned that no matter how much money one has, deep inside, we are all similar to one another.

Around then, I did a calculation showing that, even if I paid as much as I could each month, with my current pay and the interest rates on my credit cards, I would be in debt for the rest of my life. I felt overwhelmed. I considered consumer credit counseling, which could have helped me renegotiate my interest rates and even reduce my total debt.

Consumer credit counseling would have been a great option, as it would have prevented a bankruptcy from appearing on my credit report. In fact, after repaying the debt, my credit rating may have improved. If I had known how things were about to change for me, I might have gone that route.

I had dug a pretty big hole for myself before I swallowed my pride and accepted my father's kind offer to move back in with him. This temporary retreat gave me time to figure things out, file for bankruptcy, pay off my remaining debt, build up some savings, and start again. At first, I had no credit cards, partly because all I could get was a debit card. After a while, I became accustomed to paying cash all the time, and I started to like not owing anything. The habit of strictly controlling my use of debt to no more than I could pay off each month was a good beginning.

Turning Setbacks into Stepping Stones

Setbacks or mistakes are not regrettable if you learn from them. Everyone has setbacks, and tremendously successful people get back up and keep going. Life is a masterclass in who you are meant to be; if you keep trying, you will keep learning and evolving.

Life offers each of us some challenges. Accept kindness when provided. Push yourself to work harder and give more. Work toward extinguishing your debt and establishing an emergency fund. Ultimately, you will make money work for you. Your goal should be to invest for the long term, accumulating real income or assets that exceed all your future expenses. In the process, you may find yourself living life on your terms.

Why Persistence Wins

If you ever felt stuck, what helped you move forward? For me, the thought that kept me going when things were tough was a principle I learned from a college math course: The probability of success increases dramatically with persistence and repeated attempts.

Imagine I blindfolded you and placed a bucket filled with 1,000 marbles, including 999 white marbles and 1 solid-gold marble. Finding the golden marble on the first try is extremely unlikely (0.1 percent).[3] Repeated attempts significantly increase your chances until, after trying five thousand times, drawing the gold marble at least once becomes extremely likely (99.3 percent).[4] Persistence transforms a rare opportunity for success into victory, so the key is persistence.

This calculation assumes that each attempt is independent and the probability remains constant. In real life, as you learn from mistakes and adapt your strategy, your chances of success may improve even further. If you improved by even 1 percent per day on average, by the end of a year, you would be 37 times better.[5]

Finding Purpose Through Service

I took a telemarketing job at IBD, the financial newspaper founded by William J. O'Neal. Although it was humbling at first, I came to value the experience. My coworkers were bright and optimistic, I respected the product, and the company's culture of positive reinforcement helped shift my outlook. I treasured a few opportunities to speak with Mr. O'Neal.

In my spare time, I volunteered for the Red Cross and found that I genuinely enjoyed helping others; that was when I began considering a career in government.

Lessons in Leadership and Integrity

I joined the army reserve and learned professionalism, focus, physical discipline, and how to live life by a code. Although basic training was hard, I felt at home there (perhaps because there was a lot of yelling). My basic training drill sergeant yelled, "You are like a sword being forged; each time you are plunged into the fire, it makes you stronger!"

1. Professionalism means being prepared, not letting your team down,

---

3. Probability of success on one draw = $1/1000 \approx .001$. Probability of failure on one draw = $1 - p = 999/1{,}000 \approx .999$.
4. Probability of failing N times in a row = $(1 - p)^N$. Probability of succeeding *at least once* in N tries = $1 - (1 - p)^N = 1 - (1 - 999/1000)^{5000} \approx 0.993$.
5. $1.01^{365} \approx 37$.

and working together despite differences. I observed how a lack of preparation could cost lives. We learned to work together, no matter how dysfunctional that might be. One day, I got into an argument with another soldier, and we nearly came to blows. The drill sergeant stopped us, and the next day, he put us on the same firing lane during target practice to teach us how much we might someday rely on each other. Each of us manually replaced used targets in front while the other held a loaded M16 rifle. If either of us really hated the other, one of us would not have walked away that day, so I saw how petty our prior argument had been. It is not always easy, but "by working together, pooling our resources and building on our strengths, we can accomplish great things."[6]

2. Another lesson I learned was the value of focus. I noticed that total focus mitigated my fear. For example, a young soldier seemed scared while preparing to throw a live grenade for the first time; he dropped the grenade, killing a drill sergeant and himself. Focusing on the fear of what might happen is debilitating. Instead, maintaining total focus on one activity intended to achieve your objective can eliminate or significantly reduce your fear.

3. Additionally, drill sergeants taught me physical discipline by showing me that our bodies are capable of more than our minds think they are. I started training as a slow runner but pushed myself on the initial assessment, and somehow, I ended up in the fast group for daily training. I felt bad, as we all did, that we had to do push-ups every time I fell behind; by the end of training, I was running three miles in twenty-one minutes, and no one was doing push-ups because of me.

6. Ronald Reagan's remarks at the White House ceremony marking the beginning of the Summer Youth Employment Program, delivered on May 17, 1984, https://www.reaganlibrary.gov/.

4. Finally, and most importantly, I learned that living by a code (i.e., your values) is comforting because it provides inner peace, turns chaos into clarity, transforms fear into discipline, and provides direction. Saint Augustine wrote, "Peace is the tranquility of order," and living by your values provides that order.

After coming back from training, I considered active duty or joining the police or fire departments. I wanted a government job that I knew would allow me to finish my military obligation. Additionally, I wanted reliability and proximity to my newborn son.

Finding My Purpose

Amid many applicants, I felt lucky when I was hired by the SEC through its outstanding scholar program, primarily because of my grades in finance. The SEC is the US federal agency responsible for protecting investors, maintaining fair and orderly markets, and facilitating capital formation. The SEC has long pursued cases against firms that engaged in churning. Churning is the practice of excessively trading client accounts to generate commissions rather than to benefit investors. Policies like the ones I witnessed during my brokerage interviews encouraged churning. SEC cases underscored for me the importance of ethical standards in financial markets. The SEC was a blessing and a good fit, and immediately after the interview, I thought to myself, "I could see myself working there for twenty years."

At the SEC, I found honorable people who shared my passion for finance and my keen sense of ethics. My moral compass was not a liability at the SEC; to the contrary, it helped me detect fraud. I was proud and passionate to pursue their mission to protect investors. I also witnessed many successful and unsuccessful investors over the years and interviewed many successful portfolio managers. Additionally, I reviewed the accounts of scammed investors and pursued available remedies, both quietly and aggressively. Regulation primarily benefits future investors by enabling them to avoid scams or poor investments through transparent disclosures.

Many investors lost money because they failed to learn, made mistakes, or were willing and able to take risks but did not read the disclosures. Knowing the pain and uncertainty that monetary loss can create, my heart broke every time I reviewed an account that had lost a significant amount. Additionally, after investors lost money, it was hard to recover. Many investors ignored the SEC's efforts to protect them through investor alerts, free resources, press releases, and stock suspensions. So I became aware of the importance of investor education, which is why I participated in the SEC's outreach efforts; I found that educating investors also protects them.

Lessons from War

I vividly remember driving to work on September 11, 2001. It was dark in the early morning, and I listened to the first reports about the World Trade Center attacks on the car radio. My boss told me to go home for fear of another attack in Los Angeles. I felt shaken, unsettled, and determined to help in whatever way I could. When I walked through the door, my family and I held each other and wept as we tried to grasp the scale of the innocent lives lost, and we comprehended that I might soon be called away.

For many of us, September 11, 2001, marked a turning point. It reminded us that strength alone does not always prevent harm, and that even sincere diplomacy can fail. Words matter, but they are not always enough. When deterrence breaks down and peaceful options are exhausted, nations may have to resort to force to protect lives and restore the possibility of peace.

Several years later, I deployed for Operation Iraqi Freedom. Service members make personal sacrifices that only they know about. After feeling elated on our honeymoon, my new wife and I grew distant over a yearlong deployment. My son asked me, "Why did you have to go?" I struggled to explain it in terms a young boy would understand. My personal sacrifice was the distance from those I loved most.

At war, I felt deep sorrow when attending funerals for young soldiers who had barely begun their lives, and anger toward those who had killed them. Once violence is set in motion, it gathers its own momentum. Fear, grief, anger, and duty can pull people into a chain of actions and reactions. Breaking that cycle is never simple. It demands courage, discipline, and the willingness of both sides to choose a different path.

I also learned that peace becomes possible when kindness, respect, and justice outweigh the urge to strike back. I once heard about a captain who gave shoes to some Iraqi children; that simple act of humanity later saved lives when those same children warned his team of danger. Stories like that reminded me that, even in conflict, compassion can open doors that force never will. When leaders and ordinary people commit to that truth, the cycle can be interrupted, and the possibility of peace becomes real.

My experience in the Middle East helped me understand what General Douglas MacArthur meant when he said, "The soldier above all others prays for peace, for it is the soldier who must suffer and bear the deepest wounds and scars of war."[7]

My Downward Spiral

When I returned home, I completed a bodybuilding contest based on the fitness level I'd obtained in the Middle East, but the distraction was short-lived. It helped to stave off my anger, restlessness, sleep disturbances, and isolating mindset. Like falling dominoes, those patterns affected my personal relationships, and I neglected to repair the distance created by my deployment. When my first marriage ended, that loss deepened the struggles I had avoided. Speaking with other veterans made me realize how easily anyone could slip into a downward spiral if they don't have support.

7. *Veterans of Foreign Wars*, https://vfw1833.org/.

Changing My Perspective

I went to counseling through the US Department of Veterans Affairs (VA), not because I was weak, but because I finally understood that healing sometimes requires a change in perspective, not just time.[8] The process was humbling, but it kept me grounded, employed, and moving forward one day at a time. VA counseling helped me recognize that I am responsible for my thoughts, feelings, and actions. What follows is how I rebuilt my perspective and my life.

I changed my thinking through presence, forgiveness, and gratitude.

1. **Presence:** If you cannot help but think negative thoughts, positive activities may give you temporary relief. Seeing the humor in a situation is a great relief. Furthermore, activities that require intense concentration may be positive diversions and provide a reprieve. Any activity that takes you out of your head may provide respite. Ultimately, you will have to address your thoughts, but in the meantime, temporary relief is better than nothing.

2. **Forgiveness:** Forgiveness is key to living a full life, and it can be granted not just to others for any perceived wrongs, but to ourselves when we fall short of expectations. I chose to repent for the times when I did not follow my values. When I truly forgave others and myself, I felt a sense of relief.

3. **Gratitude:** I chose to see myself as lucky. I thought of my many blessings. Even difficulties taught me valuable lessons such as what does not work or what not to do. I chose to be grateful for the opportunities and lessons. Fear taught me that it has more bark than bite. Even death taught me to appreciate life; to be at peace with my mortality, and to honor those who had passed by living my life fully. I expressed gratitude, and it washed away my negative feelings.

---

8. *US Department of Veterans Affairs*, https://www.va.gov/.

Your reasoning will almost assuredly be different from mine; however, if you can see any positive lesson or higher purpose, then *choose* to focus on that thought, which will affect your feelings and actions. Choosing to forgive and be grateful was key; it changed my perspective and the trajectory of my life.

Becoming an Expert

On December 11, 2008, Bernie Madoff was arrested for the largest Ponzi scheme in history. Although it was an embarrassment for the SEC, the scandal motivated me to become an expert. I recognized how difficult it can be to detect lies; however, I promised myself that I would never miss fraud for a lack of effort or expertise.

While I was off duty, I improved my skills to do my best in support of the SEC's mission. A couple of colleagues held the CFA designation, and I respected their incredible expertise and knowledge in finance. This inspired me to study for the CFA, which comprises three levels or tests. The CFA tests were humbling because I had come to think that I was smart and knew finance very well. Even so, I failed twice before ultimately passing all three levels. I earned certifications in compliance, fraud detection, and data science.[9] Finally, I took classes in accounting, Python, and writing. During one writing course, I drafted a paper that became the basis for this book.

All Careers End Someday

On March 31, 2025, I retired at age fifty-four under Voluntary Early Retirement Authority (VERA) after twenty-five years at the SEC. VERA was bittersweet, and after so many years of striving to reach retirement, I surprisingly had mixed emotions. While I would have happily served five more years, I was also excited about retirement. Taking early retirement was possible because I was financially independent, thanks to an early pension; a small inheritance; aggressive saving;

9. While employed by the SEC, I studied while I was off duty and earned the following certifications: Chartered Financial Analyst (CFA), Certified Fraud Examiner (CFE) from the Association of Certified Fraud Examiners (ACFE), Certified Regulatory Compliance Professional (CRCP) from FINRA's Institute, and the Data Science for Investment Professionals Certificate from the CFA Institute.

and investing in stocks, mutual funds, exchange-traded funds (ETFs), and real estate. VERA appeared to be properly executed through executive authority, so I decided it was my time to move on because I was ready for a change and I knew that nobody was irreplaceable. Although reaching financial independence took longer than I'd imagined in my twenties, I've had a rich life filled with lessons, pride, and adventures, which has given me peace I would not otherwise have known.

Finding Purpose Again

It took a few months of meditation and managing my investments to realize that not only did I want to help investors, but I also needed more than the reclusive life of a writer. After a few months of drafting this book, I missed interacting with people, so I started a real estate business to stay active and help others.

Your Journey Starts Here

Thinking creatively and positively, and acting on those thoughts, helps us overcome obstacles. Fear may stop us from making investments, while greed may convince us to make ones we should not. Plans can go awry, but even mistakes can teach us valuable lessons. The Chinese symbol for crisis also means opportunity, likely because a crisis often creates an opportunity.

By picking up this book, you've taken a crucial step toward achieving financial freedom. Financial freedom means living with the peace that your assets or income exceed all your future expenses. It's the ultimate freedom to retire, travel, donate, relax, start a business, or pursue any dream, while confidently meeting your obligations. It's about working to thrive, not just to survive.

If you have a burning desire for freedom and possibilities, let's begin this journey together. Turn the page, and let's awaken your financial STAR.

PART ONE:
THE STAR METHOD

CHAPTER ONE:

What Is STAR?

STAR is an acronym to help you remember the path to financial freedom (see Table 1). You'll encounter this term throughout the book. So let's talk about what it means, and how to achieve financial freedom by focusing on just four things: saving, time, assets, and returns (STAR).

Table: 1 STAR
S = Save
T = Take time
A = Add assets, and
R = Realize net real risk-adjusted returns

- **S**: Save and invest a portion of your income;
- **T**: Take the time necessary to let your savings compound and grow exponentially;
- **A**: Add or allocate to assets that provide income or reduce expenses; and
- **R**: Receive net real risk-adjusted returns.

STAR consists of the components of a future value formula, so each element is essential to your future wealth. Your future wealth is the compounded value of your scattered, uneven contributions, the assets you already hold, and any returns.[10] You will be financially free when the future value of your assets exceeds all your future expenses. Here are several online calculators that come close to capturing this concept: Vanguard,[11] Calculator Soup,[12] and calculator.net.[13] However, nothing can capture the power of your imagination, so dare to dream, and the results may exceed your expectations.

When combined, the elements of STAR result in our future savings. We can control our assets, savings rate, time until retirement, and (to some extent) average real returns. Although wealth can be pursued through countless strategies, all of them rely on the same underlying principle—compounding—and most compounding formulas contain the same four elements: savings, time, assets, and returns (STAR). If you majored in finance, the future value of money would be one of the very first formulas you would learn. However, most people never understand the power or simplicity of building wealth. It is not difficult to understand. Depending on your circumstances, it may be challenging to execute, but it is possible. You will need to act, persist, and be patient.

STAR provides the building blocks or rules for building wealth, and its elements are not optional if you want to increase your net worth. Saving a portion of your income will increase your assets. Assets that generate cash flow or reduce your expenses will increase your income and, as a result, your savings. Striving for real, risk-adjusted returns increases the likelihood and frequency with which your assets will produce income. Finally, the longer you follow these principles, the more your wealth will grow.

Developing and sticking to a plan is like mapping out the road you will take

---

10. Future value of current assets + future value of irregular contributions. $FV = PV0\ (1 + r)^{N} + \sum Ct\ (1 + r)^{(N - t)}$

11. "Retirement Income Calculator," *Vanguard*, https://investor.vanguard.com/tools-calculators/retirement-income-calculator.

12. "Future Value of Cash Flows Calculator," *Calculator Soup*, https://www.calculatorsoup.com/calculators/financial/future-value-cash-flows-calculator.php.

13. *Calculator.net*, https://www.calculator.net/.

on a trip. Determine your savings and comfort with risk. Short-term goals will help you gauge your progress and should include monthly and yearly objectives. Start investing now. Hire a professional to assist you, or choose investments on your own. The road is clear, but the journey will pose challenges, distractions, and detours. Stay close to the road, and you will achieve financial freedom.

Now I realize that I could have achieved financial freedom more quickly, and I would like to share my ways with you. I spent years studying finance and real estate, and these are the areas where I can assist you. By helping others, I feel a sense of connection, satisfaction, and inspiration.

Your Financial Freedom Tree

What would you choose if I offered you either a million dollars or a penny that doubled every day for a month? The first time I heard that question, I got the answer wrong, but it fascinated me nonetheless. If you chose the penny option, you would have $10,737,418 in thirty days. That puzzling result demonstrated to me the power of compounding.

The secret to building wealth is not new; it has been around for ages. The tactics may change, but the formula remains the same. Ancient quotes show that these are timeless principles. The Babylonians called it interest on interest. A stone tablet carved between 1700 and 2000 BC posed the question of how long it would take for the value of a loan to double.[14]

Achieving financial freedom is a more worthwhile and enduring goal than merely accumulating money. When your assets are sufficient to cover your expenses for the rest of your life, you are financially free. Experience and education taught me how to achieve financial independence over time, and I would like to help you find a faster way.

Napoleon Hill's book *Think and Grow Rich* emphasized the power of our thoughts and imaginations in achieving success. Books like *Think and Grow Rich* may help you think in unconventional ways. Mr. Hill encouraged readers

---

14. *Tablet AO 6770*, The Louvre, Paris.

to visualize their goals and use autosuggestion to train their subconscious minds. Autosuggestion is the practice of repeating something to oneself. It is the psychological phenomenon in which a person influences their own thoughts, behaviors, or feelings through self-directed affirmations or statements. It's a form of self-talk that can shape one's mindset or attitude. For example, repeating positive affirmations like "I can do this" may help foster confidence and resilience.

By focusing on desire, faith, and persistence, *Think and Grow Rich* inspired readers to think beyond conventional boundaries and explore innovative ways to achieve their ambitions. Similarly, I encourage you to think creatively and focus on compounding in your financial life to realize your dreams.

By thinking creatively while reading *Awaken Your Financial STAR*, you may invent new, unique, innovative ways to reach your specific goals. Your inspired ideas might be variations of ideas discussed here, or even innovative ideas not covered in this book. The elements of STAR are general, timeless principles, but they are not specific to your unique circumstances. By clearly understanding the principles that build wealth, then imagining how they apply to your life, you will find a plan that works for you.

Establishing financial freedom is like planting a tree and letting it grow. Fertilize your financial tree with your dreams, desires, and determination so it may develop. Financial freedom covers necessities, but why stop there? Dream big.

Plant a seed by envisioning your life with financial independence. Thoughts are like seeds that evolve into energy, feelings, and actions. Set realistic, urgent, measurable, and specific goals. Each day, focus your energy like a laser beam on the tasks that will bring you closer to your goals. That relentless, high-energy focus will make you unstoppable. Many of the most successful people in the world focus on a purpose with obsessive intensity until it has been completed. Then they move on to the next thing.

Thinking and dreaming are the roots of your financial tree. Above subsistence, invest. Exercise patience, and reinvest. These actions are the trunk of your tree. All this effort may be challenging and will require discipline. But the fruits of your labor may be more than you could have imagined. Learn from life. Earn more than you need. Invest, earn, and reinvest. The fruits from your financial tree may superficially provide toys, luxuries, and travel. However, it may also offer many intangibles that are even more valuable.

Most people would not cut down a fruit tree to use it for firewood unless necessary; most would only use its dry branches lying on the ground for firewood. In that spirit, you should avoid using your principal or core investment capital. Only use your earnings and cash flow. As hard as this may be, this allows your financial tree to continue growing.

A couple of factors, such as cash flow and discipline, affect financial independence even after achieving a high net worth. First, your cash flow needs to exceed your expenses. In addition, you'll require discipline to spend within your means. Not spending more than your income means not cutting down your financial freedom tree.

Financial independence may give you hope for the future and enable you to give to important charities. You may be able to influence others, feel more secure, pay your bills, and provide for your family. Ultimately, if your financial tree grows large enough, you may provide a lasting legacy for future generations.

Below is an image of the financial freedom tree described above. The tree's trunk contains four tasks: learning, earning, saving, and investing. The fruits of the financial tree are in the branches and may include virtually anything.

Jackfruit are one of the largest fruits in the world, capable of weighing more than forty pounds. One jackfruit can feed a small family for several days. I hope that you will grow your financial tree into a mighty jackfruit tree and use the fruits of your work and discipline to do good for others and this world.

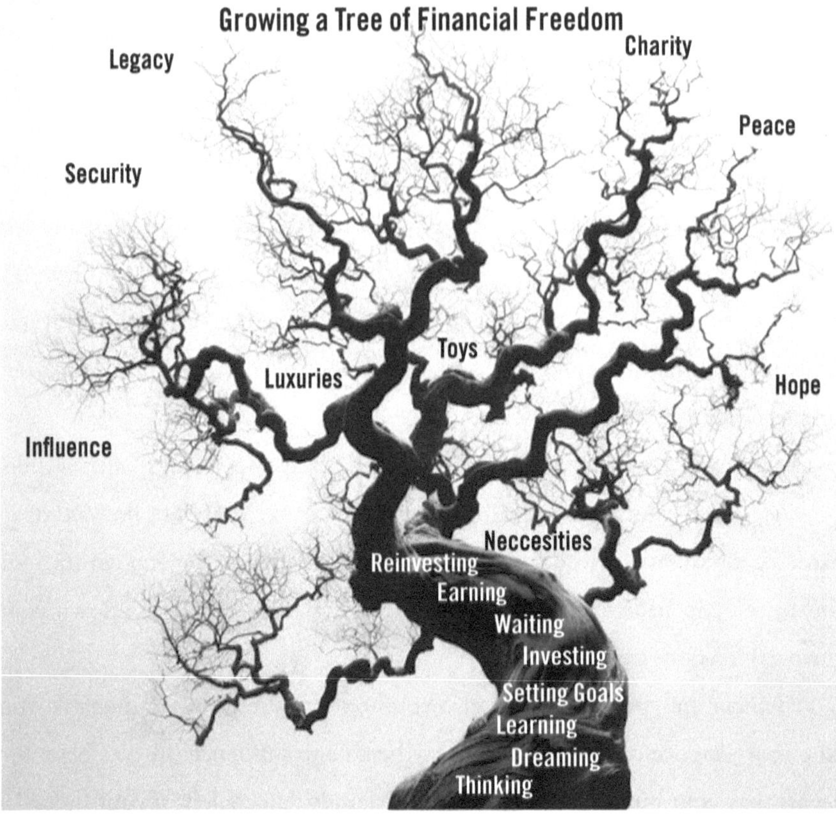

Save

Saving money is no small feat, but it is necessary. Your ability to save is the result of your net income minus your spending. You are doing well if you can save between 10 and 30 percent of your gross income.

If that feels out of reach, think about how to develop your skills or find additional work to increase your income. Create a budget by determining your necessary expenses and cutting unnecessary costs. Determine how much you can realistically save, and then save consistently.

One way to do this is by setting up an automatic savings plan. Employers, banks, and mutual funds offer automatic allotments directly from paychecks. Separate your retirement savings to make the funds less accessible. Keep your savings invested in the long term.

If you have a choice between saving money and paying off credit card debt, pay off destructive consumer debts first and save the money you would have paid in interest. Many people find it helpful to prioritize paying off high-interest debts, as this can free up resources for saving and investing. Avoid using credit cards unless you can pay them off in full each month. If this is too difficult, cut them up and discard them entirely. After my bankruptcy, I did not have credit cards for a while. Here are three ways to do this:

1. Pay cash

2. Use a debit card

3. Set up a cash-secured credit card

If you are saving and have mastered the use of credit cards, what is next?

Take Time

Do not underestimate what you can achieve in the long term. Time is the most potent factor in compounding interest, so extending your investment horizon also increases your possible returns. Your investment horizon is the time period until you need the money invested or have reached your goal. For example, let's say you are saving for a car. You want to buy the car in one year, so your investment horizon is one year. Longer investment horizons allow for greater compounding. Over time, your principal may grow exponentially. Expanding your investment horizon sounds simple, but market fluctuations make it difficult to focus on the long term.

You want exponential growth, and with time and positive returns, that's what you will get. As your capital grows, so will your gains and losses. A 10 percent gain or loss is more emotional when you have ten million dollars than when you have ten thousand dollars because it's a significant percentage of your income.

Maintaining control over your emotions will help you stay invested during fluctuations. Investors may overreact when they experience uncertainty, fear, or greed, which leads to market volatility. Clearly understand your investments. This will help you make better decisions, and it may help you stay on course during volatility. It is not necessary to beat the markets.

Avoid glamorous investments. A glamorous investment is one that everyone knows about and generally desires. Glamorous investments tend to be expensive. The problem is that the price reflects grand expectations, so if anything goes wrong, your investment will underperform. People compete for great investments, just as they do for great jobs. Be careful if everyone is buying or if someone is trying hard to sell you an investment. Financial markets constantly change, so what worked before may not work in the future. Past performance is not a guarantee of future results. Sometimes, yesterday's best returns are today's riskiest investments, so avoid chasing the latest fad.

Given enough time, slow and steady wins the race. The investor who consistently and methodically purchases low-cost equity index funds or exchange-traded funds is likely to have more to show for their efforts than someone who is chasing get-rich-quick schemes.

Allocate Assets

An asset generates cash, and a liability consumes cash. The worth of an asset is equal to its future cash flow (including growth) minus any inflation-induced loss. If your assets require continuous cash payments, you are not financially free because you must continue to work. So you want to maximize assets that generate or save more cash than they use.

Take a moment to consider your assets and liabilities. Is your car an asset or a liability? It generates expenses, so it is a liability to the extent that you do not use it for work, and you should try to minimize the cost. Is your house an asset or a liability? Your house can reduce long-term expenses and generate cash flow. However, while you are living there, you spend more than the house brings in. If you live in a bigger house than you need, it is a liability. Living beyond your means will make it difficult to achieve financial freedom. Saving money will become easier if you demand value from your expenses and income from your assets.

Receive Real Risk-Adjusted Returns

The real risk-adjusted return is the net return you can expect after accounting for the risk you are taking, including inflation, volatility, and other factors. The inflation rate depreciates a currency's future value, so the actual or real return is the return you get, excluding inflation. The real return reflects the actual return in today's dollars. The risk-adjusted return estimates the highest return for a given level of risk by measuring and comparing risk to reward. Let's discuss two examples to make it clear how important this is.

1. Inflation matters. Two investments offer the same amount of cash flow; however, the first investment increases in value with inflation, and the other does not. In this example, you are better off with the investment that increases with inflation over the long term. Over thirty years, the inflation-protected investment will nearly triple (i.e., 2.8 times) at 3.5 percent inflation. On the other hand, the financial investment that will not increase with inflation will be worth about one third (34 percent) of the initial investment. For example, the investor who purchased a rental property instead of bonds with the exact initial yield over thirty years will be 8.23 times (2.8/0.34) better off at the end of thirty years.

2. Volatility matters. Would you rather have 50 percent returns or 5 percent returns? Well, it depends. Generally, higher returns involve greater risks, including volatility. How likely and consistent are the returns? Assume the 5 percent returns are very consistent. Alternatively, if you make 50 percent one year and lose 34 percent the next year, you'll earn more with the consistent 5 percent investment. When you lose money, you need higher returns to recover your losses. While higher-return investments are generally more volatile, inconsistent returns may result in lower average returns than those

of alternative investments; therefore, it is essential to invest rather than speculate. In other words, you want to be sure that your long-term expected return is positive (that is, you don't lose money).

Check Your Knowledge

1. What does STAR stand for?
2. What is the real risk-adjusted return?
3. Why should you think creatively while reading *Awaken Your Financial STAR*?

Chapter Summary/Key Takeaways

- STAR is an acronym to help you remember the road to financial freedom: Save (S) and, over time (T), you will build your assets (A) with real risk-adjusted returns (R). When the present value of your future expenses (adjusted for inflation) is less than the present value of your assets at your average rate of return, you are financially free. Alternatively, you are financially free when you have reliable, real, passive net income that exceeds your expenses.
- The real risk-adjusted return is the net return you can expect after accounting for the risk you are taking, including inflation, volatility, etc.
- There are many ways to achieve financial freedom, so thinking for yourself will enable you to see different paths. By doing so, you may invent new, unique, innovative ways to reach your specific goals.

CHAPTER TWO:

Navigate with STAR

Money is a terrible master but an excellent servant.
—P. T. Barnum

Reginald Lewis's Mindset and Work Ethic

Reginald Lewis grew up in a working-class, middle-class family in East Baltimore, Maryland, but he became a billionaire. Mr. Lewis's parents instilled a strong work ethic and emphasized the importance of education. Reginald Lewis was a lawyer, corporate raider, and self-made billionaire who appeared on the 1993 *Forbes* 400 list of the wealthiest Americans. Mr. Lewis began writing an excellent autobiography, *Why Should White Guys Have All the Fun?*[15] However, Blair S. Walker completed the biography when Mr. Lewis passed away.

Mr. Lewis possessed an exceptional work ethic. During college, he worked nights and weekends as a photographer's sales assistant. He worked so hard and generated so much business that he was offered a partnership, all while graduating on the dean's list. Upon graduating from Harvard University, Paul, Weiss, Rifkind, Wharton & Garrison—one of the most elite New York law firms—hired him straight out of school. Top firms only recruited students who were at the top of their class *in performance, reputation, or both.*

Mr. Lewis established his law firm just two years after graduating from

15. Reginald F. Lewis and Blair S. Walker, *Why Should White Guys Have All the Fun?* (1995).

Harvard Law School. He left Paul, Weiss, Rifkind, Wharton & Garrison after two years because he believed he could build something bigger on his own. With few steady clients and little savings, Mr. Lewis turned to his uncle Paul, who loaned him money to cover his living expenses and early business costs. This cash flow enabled him to hustle for clients, build a reputation, take on civil rights cases, grow a corporate practice, and eventually transition into dealmaking.

Mr. Lewis built a successful law firm over fifteen years and ultimately achieved financial freedom. He then grew that wealth to over a billion dollars by conducting several leveraged buyouts (i.e., he purchased entire companies using debt), utilizing the knowledge and money he had gained in his law firm. Mr. Lewis worked extremely hard and was shocked that the media portrayed him as an overnight success.

Having financial freedom means your assets or income exceed all your future living expenses. Your real passive income exceeds your real future uses. Financial freedom is a battle between average after-tax returns and real average costs. Once you have obtained financial independence, you are free to pursue your dreams without financial worries. In Mr. Lewis's life, this meant playing the leveraged buyout game and becoming a billionaire.

If you want extreme wealth, your path may not be easy because, like Mr. Lewis, you will have to stay focused and work hard. Having the right mindset is essential to achieve anything in life, and knowing the STAR principles alone will not make you wealthy. You will need to believe in your vision, set goals, learn, earn, save, and invest. With persistence and time, anything is possible. So this chapter covers how to master your mindset.

You Are the STAR of This Movie, So What Is Your Starting Scene?

Imagine you are the star of a movie and you're hiking in the wilderness with a map and a compass. To reach your destination, you need to know where you are. First, you identify landmarks. Next, you orient your map using a compass to ensure you're going where you want to go. Having figured out where you are and where you are going, you plot the most direct route to your destination, taking terrain into account. You avoid unnecessary risks (like snowed-in passes or terrain you might not have the skill or equipment to navigate, like rappelling over cliffs). All the while you watch the landmarks as you progress on your journey.

You can apply these same principles as you're navigating your financial journey. Of course, your financial landscape will look a little different than the wilderness. It will include your debts, short-term and long-term needs, assets, net monthly cash flow, and available returns. Based on your financial position, it should be clear whether you are missing assets, savings, time, or returns. You're the star of this movie, so let's set the scene.

- **S:** How much can you reasonably save, given your income and necessary expenses?
- **T:** How much time do you have until you will need the money you invest?
- **A:** What are your assets and liabilities?
- **R:** Finally, consider what the current investment landscape looks like and what you can reasonably expect to receive in returns.

If you are not already financially free, you lack savings, time, assets, or returns (STAR). After assessing your financial situation, what you lack may be clear, but figuring out how to overcome personal obstacles may not be. For now, just understanding the problem is a big part of the solution.

Savings: What Are Your *Necessary* Expenses?

Your expenses require payment; which expenses should you plan for to achieve financial independence? Your necessities include food, water, clothing, shelter, and medical care. Your discretionary expenses include your wants, so the sky is the limit. It is easy to confuse wants with necessities. Your expenses will increase with inflation. If your income rises with fixed costs, you will have additional money to spend on other things.

While I was in the army, I realized that I did not need much money. The army provided food, shelter, uniforms, and medical care. So, despite not making much money, I was able to save. Consider the minimum standards and costs required to cover your basic living requirements. For shelter, can you get by with less space, take roommates, etc.? Clothes do not have to be expensive; they have to be functional.

If you only plan for your basic needs, you may feel unfulfilled and unmotivated. So I encourage you to dream.

Time: What Is Your Investment Horizon?

Your investment horizon is the time remaining to achieve your goals. Generally, the shorter the time, the less risk you should take, because short-term declines may result in not reaching your goal. On the other hand, you can afford to take more risks with longer-term goals because riskier assets will have time to recover and may offer higher returns, making it easier to achieve a given goal.

Assets

Your assets consist of everything you own, including your skills. Your skills affect your income, which increases your savings potential and, in turn, your assets. Your assets generate more income via returns. Furthermore, returns will build your assets at an exponential rate. Your skills, assets, savings, and returns all work together like a self-reinforcing cycle to make you wealthier. Can you see why some get richer?

Money itself is a convenient exchange method and only has value because we agree that it does. You may feel wealthier if you have more nominal money, but if you are spending more, you may not be.

Even the Roman Empire inflated its currency, and our governments are unlikely to stop inflating ours. Some assets decline in value with inflation, while others appreciate. Your debt and bonds fall in value with inflation. Stocks, too, benefit from low inflation. Some assets (such as precious metals, real estate, and specific stocks) benefit from high inflation.

Sustainable yield is the amount that you can remove from an investment without depleting it over time. So sustainable yield is the real return less whatever you take out. When the sustainable yield on your assets exceeds your expenses, you are financially free. Like Reginald Lewis, you can use this freedom to propel you to unimaginable heights. So your goal is to obtain a cash flow that adjusts for inflation and is sufficient to cover your living expenses.

Returns: Is Your Required Return Realistic Given Market Returns?

Your portfolio's required return rate is the return necessary to achieve your goals for your time horizon. You should consider whether this required return is realistic relative to the historical returns of what you choose to invest in.

Vision and Inspiration

People find inspiration in countless ways, including meditation, prayer, time in nature, creative expression, and moments of quiet reflection. The wisdom you discover connects you to the universe, which is constantly changing. The formula for wealth and the words on these pages will not change; however, you and the world around you will continue to evolve. If you are open, wisdom and insight can come from many sources, so each moment brings new possibilities for understanding. Here is the technique I use to find inspiration.

Find a quiet spot that brings you peace, and meditate for a while. I find contentment at the beach, listening to the sounds of the ocean. If you are in a safe place, close your eyes and concentrate on your breathing and the present moment. Try to quiet your mind and forget your worries. There is no yesterday or tomorrow, only now. The noises you hear are not distractions; they are the reality of the present moment. Feel your skin, sense the air; focus on this instant. You have access to a much more powerful source of wisdom and knowledge than I could ever place on these pages. It is in these moments of quiet reflection when I feel most inspired. While feeling inspired, think about your life and the elements of STAR. What element do you need to build on to improve your life and this world? Be persistent, be patient, and have faith in your vision for a better future.

Setting Goals: RUMS

Dreams are visions you create that can take shape, but goals require focus and actions. To achieve financial freedom, you'll need to choose goals that are: realistic, urgent, measurable, and specific (RUMS). All your goals should be specific and measurable so that you can determine whether you have met them. Your short-term goals should also be realistic and urgent because they require daily activities.

RUMS goals are more effective than just having fuzzy goals or dreams. For example, let us say you want to lose weight. You envision yourself as a thin person, and you set a goal to lose weight. Stopping there, you may never achieve your vision. By contrast, let's say you think you would look your best if you were fifty-two pounds lighter than you are now. On the surface, this would seem like a challenging goal.

Let's break the goal down and use backward planning to determine what you would need to do today. To lose fifty-two pounds in a year, you would need to lose one pound a week. One pound of fat holds about 3,500 calories. So you'd need to calculate your total daily energy expenditure (TDEE) and determine the appropriate calorie deficit based on your current weight, activity level, and other factors. You'd then need to eat a 500-calorie deficit each day to gradually reach your goal. You could use this process for virtually any goal. If I wanted to learn to play piano, I'd practice for five or ten minutes daily. If I wanted to pass a test, I'd study a certain amount daily and weekly.

To set your RUMS goals, you'll first need to evaluate your financial situation, calculate your net monthly savings after all expenses, and determine how close you are to financial freedom. Next, identify your goals. Set clear milestones that you believe in but are challenging.

Your short-term goals should be realistic and urgent, with daily, weekly, or monthly deadlines. Set weekly or monthly goals to earn and save more. Set goals that move you toward your long-term goals and stretch you but are realistic. For example, I set a goal of writing one hour per day to author this book.

Set a specific date to achieve financial freedom, with measurable yearly milestones that serve as your long-term financial goals.

Long-Term Goals

Money can buy freedom, houses, cars, experiences, security, power, etc. It is a versatile tool that can enable you to do many things. What you do with your money may even inspire others to love you. But I assure you, it is not truly the money you want. Money is just a medium of exchange. Whatever it is that you want, focus on that, and use money as a tool to achieve your dreams in a smart way.

When I was a child, my favorite teacher was Sister Mary Ann. Sister Mary Ann was joyful and fun; all the children liked her. I was not a particularly good student because I was always daydreaming. I dreamt of far-off places and things that I imagined myself doing. One day, Sister Mary Ann whispered, "Dreamers never achieve anything." I was devastated for a while, thinking she was telling me that I, a dreamer, would never do anything with my life. It took me years to realize that she was right. She was right, but what she said was incomplete.

Dreamers are blessed with vision but may never act on it; visionaries make their visions a reality by combining courage, confidence, discipline, and perseverance. Like a sculptor working with clay, dreamers must sculpt themselves into visionaries by finding dreams that they are passionate about and taking action.

Connect with your inner child and determine what you genuinely want from life. If you want freedom, you must learn to balance living within your means and following your other dreams. You do not have to sacrifice your dreams to achieve financial independence. Visualize your ideal life. Work to achieve financial freedom by incorporating what you want in life.

Being financially free will allow you a degree of independence. For example, being financially free gives you the ability to say "F— off" when your employer does something that would crush your soul if you stayed.

Before I retired, I met a charming lady named Sharon at a party. Sharon was partially retired and super excited about the nonprofit organizations she volunteered for. She advised me, "Before you retire, find what you are retiring to. If you retire, you will fill your time, but you may find yourself unfulfilled." To ensure that you have a clear vision for your future, find something you are passionate about and wake up excited to do every day.

If you have a clear sense of your purpose, your long-term goals will quickly follow. Praying, meditating, or focusing on the meaning of your life can help you gain clarity. Consider your legacy. How do you want people to remember you? Allow yourself to dream, and envision your life without any restrictions.

Now think for a moment about the following questions that only you can answer:

- Who do you want to be?
- What gets you excited about life?
- Why do you want money and/or financial freedom?
- What will you do when you retire?
- Where do you want to live when you retire?
- When do you want to retire?

These questions may help you develop your goals, but they may be difficult to answer. Your reasons for wanting success will keep you determined. Knowing your destination increases your likelihood of getting there, so try to visualize your ideal future.

A vision board is a visual representation of your goals. Create a vision board with pictures that represent your long-term goals. Your vision will be influenced by when you want to retire, the strategies you need to employ, the quality of your retirement, the years you have left, and the milestones you set. At some point, you may find yourself with substantial wealth. Since none of us will get out of life alive, estate planning will help reduce taxes and legal fees for the people and/

or organizations that are important to you. Estate planning differs from country to country and changes over time, so it's best to consult an attorney.

Envisioning Retirement

To determine what you'll need for retirement, you need to determine the annual cost of the lifestyle you want. Realistically, how much do your necessities (such as food, clothing, transportation, utilities, rent, or mortgage) cost? Your necessities determine your minimum income. Additionally, how much will your desired luxuries cost? In today's dollars, what amount do you want to spend on travel, cars, boats, airplanes, and entertainment? The more luxuries you desire, the more you will need. Adding up your necessities and luxuries will give you your total yearly expenses in retirement. Your long-term goals should also be specific and measurable. To achieve financial freedom, your passive income must exceed your expenses, or your assets must be sufficient so that you will never run out of money.

The most straightforward and secure retirement plan would be to exceed your total annual expenses with real (inflation-adjusted) income, such as passive income from real estate. Using the income method is the simplest, but it can be harder to achieve. We can determine the income to strive for by adding up the annual cost of the lifestyle you want. This is the amount of actual, real passive income you should strive for. If you are investing in productive assets that appreciate with inflation (i.e., equities or real estate), the value and income from those assets should also rise over time.

Alternatively, you could estimate how much money would allow you to live the rest of your life without worrying about financial concerns. This approach would include trying to obtain an amount that should last you throughout the rest of your life.

A simple method to estimate this amount is to take the annual income goal for the lifestyle you desire, and divide it by 3 percent; this is the net worth (excluding your residence) you should strive for to live indefinitely if invested in stocks and real estate. Many people attempt to estimate a lower required net worth based on their life expectancy, which can lead to difficulties if they live longer.[16] Another way to address longevity risk would be to include a safety reserve or an additional amount above what you need for retirement, such as your home equity. This may be an asset you can tap into if you outlive your savings. Still another approach is to buy an annuity and request annuitization, which provides a guaranteed income stream for the rest of your life. Furthermore, delaying retirement or reducing spending will reduce the likelihood that your portfolio will be exhausted. Although there are diverse ways of calculating the amount you'll need, all of them have uncertainty due to the number of variables that cannot be determined. Whether you choose the income or net worth method, you have a long-term goal to strive for, and you will be financially free when you reach either. Given the uncertainty, I think dividing your desired income by 3 percent is conservative but overly simplistic.

Keep in mind that everyone's situation is different, so any rule of thumb (like withdrawing 3 percent) is inherently flawed. The real historical geometric average annual equity return over 142 years was 6.3 percent.[17] A 3 to 6 percent withdrawal rate while invested in equities should allow your wealth to grow indefinitely; however, as you increase your withdrawal rate, the effects of volatility will become more dramatic. Additionally, choosing less risky assets will reduce returns and may amplify inflationary effects. Finally, your age, health, and heirs affect your goals. For all these reasons, I prefer the income method.

What you invest in will affect your expected return and portfolio volatility. Increased volatility may increase the likelihood that you will run out of money. Increasing returns will typically increase volatility, too. However, higher returns and lower volatility will improve your ability to spend during retirement. My experience has been that cash flow is more stable than asset prices. So, again, using

16. Using an actuarial life table, you could estimate this amount by multiplying the present value for your anticipated spending by the difference between your retirement age and the length of your life expectancy, and adjusting for inflation and returns; however, there is a significant risk that you would outlive your savings (i.e., longevity risk).

17. "Online Data Robert Shiller," http://www.econ.yale.edu/~shiller/data.htm.

cash flow rather than total asset values may be a more conservative approach to securing your future income.

Establish a financial plan and set a retirement date. Sometimes, the asset classes you are comfortable with may differ from those needed to achieve your goals. When that is the case, you can save more, use leverage, learn about investments that can help you achieve your goals, or adjust your goals. Setting milestones can help you to keep moving toward your long-term goals. For example, set an ambitious yearly savings amount. When it makes financial sense, purchase your primary residence to reduce your annual expenses. Set an average investment return objective that is consistent with the amount of risk you are willing to take and the amount of effort you are willing to exert.

I use historical returns for each asset class to estimate my long-term expected returns. You may need leverage and/or an active management process to exceed these returns. Remember that there are no guarantees in investments, and you should be highly suspicious of anyone who claims they can guarantee returns.

Be patient and disciplined. Long-term goals require patience and discipline, and they can be challenging to achieve. That is why you should set and focus on short-term goals that are specifically designed to reach your long-term goals.

Short-Term Goals

Dwayne ("The Rock") Johnson likes to say, "Wake up determined. Go to bed satisfied." I love The Rock's winning attitude. Start small, but dream big. When you wake up totally focused on what you need to do for the day, you dramatically increase the likelihood of achieving your long-term goals. Single-mindedly working toward your daily goals makes you focus on the one thing you can truly control: what you're doing right now. So focus on today, savor your successes, and laugh at your losses. Be present with purpose.

Set a goal to earn more. If you are an employee, how can you get a raise by getting additional training or providing your employer with what they want? Do you have free time in which you could take another job or turn a hobby into a business? If you own a business, how could you sell more? Are there additional products or services that existing customers need? Since I own rentals, let us use real estate as an example. If you own a residential, vacation, or rental home, consider renting part or the entire property. Add services that may generate additional revenue, such as laundry or vending machines. Expenses (such as utility expenses) passed along to tenants increase cash flow. Bigger properties may benefit from vending machines, washers, and dryers.

Set a monthly savings goal by creating a budget. This is a great start. Gather your financial documents, including income and expense details. Calculate your monthly income to see how much money comes in. Determine the difference between what you make and what you take home. Next, review your bank and credit card statements. Create a list of your monthly expenses, including approximate averages. What costs can you reduce or eliminate? Make a goal to save a certain amount each month. Then design your daily goals to keep you on track toward your monthly savings goal. Can you change some habits? Brainstorm ways to take home more, reduce expenses, and save more.

Set aside time to reevaluate your assets and income. The goal should be to spend time evaluating your current and prospective investments, rather than achieving a specific result, because, over the short term, your results may vary significantly. Consider whether the facts have changed, which initially made an existing investment attractive. Shift assets to higher-potential-return investments only when it clearly makes sense. Additionally, consider any tax consequences of making changes. If you use a broker or advisor, you should still regularly review your financial situation and understand what they are doing.

Set goals to pay off destructive consumer debt and debt on non-income-producing assets. First, pay off your loan with the highest interest rate. Then pay the loan with the next highest interest rate. Pay off all debt for which you cannot earn more on the borrowed money than you are paying.

Set nonfinancial goals to improve the quality of your life. I Sometimes became so focused on financial goals that I forgot to enjoy the journey. There is more to life than money. Furthermore, if you are not healthy, you may not enjoy the money you have. Consider setting goals to enhance your body, mind, and spirit. Set goals to work out and eat right (i.e., maintain a healthy lifestyle). Set goals to spend time learning something you're interested in. Set aside a certain amount of time to meditate, pray, or reconnect spiritually. Short-term goals become habits when you no longer need to think about them.

Building Habits

We are what we repeatedly do. Excellence, then, is not an act, but a habit.
—Will Durant

Now that you've defined your short-term and long-term RUMS goals, you can start to chart a course of action. Actions support habits, and habits are things you do almost automatically. One of your short-term goals should be to develop excellent habits. What habits must you cultivate to become financially free? For one thing, the wealthy generally spend less than they make and invest the difference. You can also commit to continually learning and developing your skills and financial knowledge.

While striving to achieve financial independence, you will engage in four primary activities: learning, earning, saving, and investing. These four activities are my duties, what I like to call my duty to deliver. These are the things that I must do. The duty to deliver comprises investing in yourself through learning. When you earn, follow that by saving and investing. When you invest, you will learn. These activities will create a self-reinforcing cycle that, with patience, will lead you to financial freedom. Learning is the beginning and the end of the cycle. For many, learning a skill enables them to earn more than subsistence and to save the extra earnings. Once saved, invest the extra money to generate earnings to reinvest. The cycle ends with learning, as you learn from your successes and failures.

You should only invest in what you understand and continually learn. Understanding your investments is critical to preventing significant losses. In general, if you continue to learn and grow, it is only a matter of time before you will succeed. With persistence and time, even the loftiest goals are attainable. As you learn more, the investments that you understand will grow and your areas of competence will expand, enabling you to invest in new asset classes with ease and comprehension.

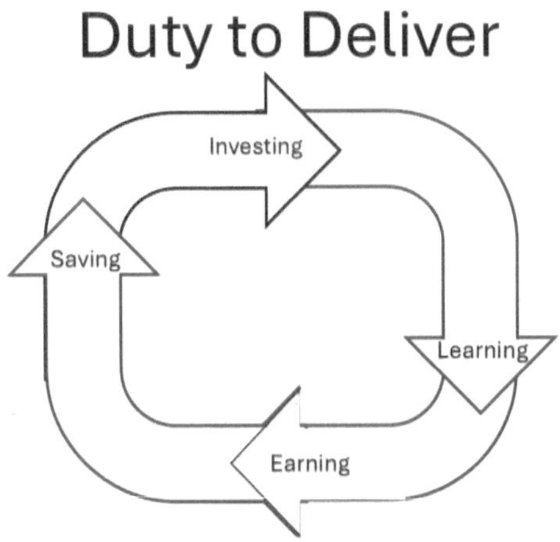

Increase your income by learning skills in traditional or unconventional ways. A formal education may help you increase your earning power if you choose a focus that gives you skills that are in demand. I love reading and listening to terrific books by the giants who came before me. Lao Tzu said in the *Tao Te Ching*, "When the student is ready, the teacher will appear." If we are open to learning from all things, we can also learn from everyday experiences, as well as from more traditional sources. Let's commit to lifelong learning and growing.

Aside from learning, focus on earning, saving, and investing. These are the things you can control. Earnings will enable you to save. Savings will allow you to invest. As you invest, you will learn and earn. So the circle of learning, earning, saving, and investing is continuous and self-reinforcing.

Your Investment Profile Based on Your Goals

Any competent advisor or broker will need to review your investment profile at the beginning of your relationship. Your investment profile includes your goals or objectives, investment horizon, age, experience, risk tolerance, tax bracket, and liquidity needs. If your broker or advisor does not require some of this information, then they may not be considering it. If you manage your own investments, considering your profile may help you determine if your plan is realistic or needs adjustment.

Without goals, you are like a ship that has set sail with no destination. While you could save and invest without specific goals and still achieve the same results, you are much more likely to reach your goals if you consciously recognize them and act. For some goals in your life, you may be able to determine the amount of money it will cost to achieve that goal. You may want to set up specific accounts to achieve individual goals; for example, you might have one account to save to send your kids to college and another to buy a home.

Separating your goals in different accounts may help you determine the appropriate risk to achieve each goal. For example, if you've already set aside enough money to send your child to college and they are almost ready to go, then you should not take much risk with those assets. Your goals and investment horizon affect the types of investments you choose.

Ultimately, you keep your after-tax returns. However, your after-tax returns drop for taxable investments as your tax bracket increases. Therefore, individuals in low tax brackets will benefit more from higher-taxed investments such as taxable interest. Additionally, a professionally trained short-term investor will keep more of the profits from flipping houses and day trading if they are in a low tax bracket. Individuals in high tax brackets will derive more value from tax-deferred and tax-exempt investments such as real estate rentals, retirement accounts, municipal bonds, and annuities.

Additionally, your *ability* and *willingness* to take risks will determine the kinds of investments you or your advisor should choose. Your *ability* to take risks refers to your capacity to withstand potential losses. What are the consequences of failure if you fail to achieve your goal? When assessing your risk-taking ability, you should consider a range of factors, such as your investment knowledge, time horizon, age, liquidity needs, and wealth. Your *willingness* to take risks refers to your preferences and reflects your values, beliefs, and goals. Your ability and willingness will change over time, but in general, the lower your ability or willingness, the longer it will take you to achieve your goals.

Market risk and return are the amount of return given at a certain level of risk. In general, the higher the expected return, the higher the risk. The following is a list of investment classes, from least risky to riskiest: cash equivalents, bonds, stocks, and alternative investments. Cash equivalents include money market funds, bank deposits, certificates of deposit, and Treasury bills. Bonds are fixed-income securities, such as government and corporate bonds, of varying qualities. Stocks are shares of ownership and vary widely in risk and potential returns, from micro-capitalization and emerging-market stocks to growth companies and mature mid- and large-capitalization stocks. Alternative investments include real estate, commodities, hedge funds, private equity, and cryptocurrencies. Remember that higher risk does not necessarily mean higher return because plenty of investments don't make sense when you consider risk-to-reward ratios.

The return you need to achieve your goals with your investment horizon is your required return. Suppose the average historical return for asset classes you are willing to invest in is lower than your portfolio's required return. In that case, you must adjust the assets invested, add savings, or expand your time horizon.

What Should You Do Before Choosing Your Investments?

If you want to choose investments yourself, discover effective investment strategies to enhance your chances of success. You'll also find several helpful investment books listed in the Further Reading section. Visit the SEC's website at https://www.investor.gov/ and read the free literature on various investment topics that may interest you. The Financial Industry Regulatory Authority (FINRA) also offers free investor publications on its website at https://www.finra.org/ that you can read to educate yourself. These organizations' missions are to protect investors. When considering real estate investments, you should thoroughly research market rents, costs, values, and property-specific risks.

Some say you make money when you buy, meaning that the work is in finding an excellent investment. Once found, you purchase it and wait. However, you can also lose money by investing; there are no guarantees. If it sounds too good to be true, it probably is. Only after fully understanding the risks should you decide whether to invest.

Know precisely what you are buying. Securities typically have prospectuses or annual reports. You should read one of these documents before making any investment purchase. Depending on the investment you are considering, you will want to look for different things. Generally, you want to understand the investment well. You should at least understand the costs, potential risks, and rewards.

Save money by using a discount broker and low-cost, no-load, broad-based index mutual funds or ETFs. Discount stock brokerages offer research and execution services but no advice. Mutual funds are diversified portfolios with passive or professional management. Mutual funds without sales charges are no-load mutual funds. Broad-based index funds track indexes such as the Standard & Poor's (S&P) 500 index or the Russell 3000 index.

Thoughts and Actions

Henry Ford said, "Whether you think you can or think you can't, you're right."

Your thoughts influence your feelings and actions; persistent thoughts often become reality. When you think you can do something, your next thought may be how you will do it. If you feel you cannot, you may stop thinking about achieving your goal entirely. Your short-term goals should be bite-size milestones that you believe you can achieve. Believe in who you are. Believe in your process and in the fact that you're heading in the right direction.

When you come up short, do not quit; instead, shift. It is easy to stay positive when you are winning; it's when you lose that you are truly being tested. My mother used to tell me, "When life hands you a lemon, make lemonade." The only failures are those who quit; the most significant successes often fail more than anyone else knows. President Abraham Lincoln was a good example because everyone knows he served as president during the American Civil War; however, few know that he lost eight elections for various positions prior to being elected as president. When life knocks you on your butt, get up as fast as you can, dust yourself off, and proceed to your destination. If your results are less than what you desired, learn from the experience and adjust your plan accordingly. Sometimes, attaining a goal may cause you to lose focus because you no longer have a goal. When you reach or exceed your objectives, shift your goals higher to maintain your focus and attention in the long term.

A former boss told me, "You need to learn to control your thoughts." At that time, I thought that was impossible. As I have grown older, I have realized that our thoughts are one of the few things we can control. Controlling your thoughts does not mean that you will never have a fleeting negative thought or doubt; however, you do not need to dwell on them. Recognize your fears and doubts, take action to counteract them if necessary, and let them go. Instead, focus on the dreams you want to create. In meditation, one technique is to focus on your breathing and nothing else. When doing this, you may find your mind wandering. This is normal. To counteract a wandering mind, you can use autosuggestion (i.e., repetitive statements), visualization, and total focus on short-term goals that move you in the right direction. In today's fantastic world of AI videos, it is easier than ever to visualize your ideal life. For example, I created an AI movie of the future life I want, and I watched it once every morning and once every night.

Check Your Knowledge

1. What is financial freedom?
2. What four characteristics should goals have?
3. What is your most direct route to financial freedom?

Chapter Summary/Key Takeaways

In this chapter, we reviewed the most direct route to financial freedom.

First, assess your current situation. Your assets consist of everything you own, including your skills. Your expenses are outflows necessary for the lifestyle you desire. Consider your investment profile, including your goals or objectives, investment horizon, age, experience, risk tolerance, tax bracket, and liquidity needs.

Second, set RUMS goals that are realistic, urgent, measurable, and specific.

Third, pay off any destructive consumer debt.

Fourth, save first to build a short-term fund, then to invest.

Fifth, observe the available returns.

Sixth, invest in the best opportunities, learn, and repeat.

CHAPTER THREE:

Save

There is a common saying that the bucket that continually adds more water than it spills eventually overflows. There are two ways to make your savings grow: 1) increase the amount of water that goes into the bucket, or 2) decrease the amount of water that goes out.

No Savings Equals No Freedom

The harsh reality is that, to achieve and keep financial freedom, more income must come in than goes out; you must save. Saving is a foundational step toward investing and building wealth. Even after reaching financial independence, many find that maintaining discipline around their spending helps preserve their freedom and peace of mind. You may have heard stories of lottery winners who went broke. If they had invested their lottery winnings in cash-flowing assets and then saved even one penny of their earnings each year (i.e., they did not spend more than they made), that likely would never have happened. So here are two polar opposite examples of why saving is so critically important.

Sylvia Bloom accumulated an eight-million-dollar portfolio on a legal secretary's salary by age ninety-six, illustrating the power of living below your means and investing wisely. Ms. Bloom was born to immigrants and grew up in Brooklyn during the Great Depression before putting herself through college. She donated her fortune to noble causes such as scholarships and her family. Ms. Bloom worked as a legal secretary for sixty-seven years and mimicked the investment methodologies of the lawyers she worked with. Reportedly, she made her money by investing in equities and living modestly. Ms. Bloom lived in a rent-controlled apartment. She dressed nicely but did not overspend. Having grown up during the Great Depression, she knew what it was like not to have money. Even her closest friends and family did not know she was wealthy. Saving even tiny amounts over time can really add up.[18]

By contrast, Warren Sapp was an NFL lineman who earned over seventy-five million dollars over his short career but ultimately filed for bankruptcy. During the bankruptcy, Mr. Sapp had to sell off nearly all his belongings. At an auction, his expensive tastes in collectibles became clear. The auction included a lion-skin rug and Muhammad Ali's gloves, among other high-value items. Sure, he had expensive tastes, but he filed for bankruptcy because he did not save and invest enough.

To achieve financial independence, the amount you keep is more important than the amount that flows through your hands. Saving is not just a habit; it is a necessity if you ever hope to be financially free, so you must find a way. Having more income than expenses is a common challenge, regardless of background. Building new habits often takes time and persistence, especially when circumstances are tough. Let's explore some creative ways to save more, even when it feels difficult.

Increasing Income Until It Overflows

Your cash flow is the amount you can save and invest. The more revenue or income you have, the more opportunities you have to save. This is true whether you own a business or work for someone. Business income can be highly tax-efficient because you spend before you pay tax, unlike employment income. Granted, there are limitations on what you can legally spend money on. Say you want a fancy car, which helps you win clients. One could argue that the business could buy or lease the car and expense part of it. If you own a business, hiring

18. Shawn M. Carter, "A 96-Year-Old Secretary Amassed a Secret $8 Million Fortune—Here's How," *CNBC*, May 8, 2018, https://www.cnbc.com/2018/05/08/how-a-96-year-old-secretary-amassed-a-secret-8-million-fortune.html.

a certified public accountant (CPA) may help you maximize your deductions without breaking the law.

Employment income is very tax-inefficient; however, there are ways to shield at least some of your income from taxes. If you are an employee, shield some of your income by choosing an employer that offers a 401(k), health savings accounts, and/or flexible spending account. These retirement and health accounts are fantastic ways to prepare for anticipated expenses. Also consider untaxed benefits that your employer pays, such as expense reimbursement, free food, lodging, etc. For example, the army offers free food and housing, enabling you to save more than you could otherwise. Some employers offer a flat rate per diem for travel, so volunteering for travel may be a terrific way to save.

Provide Utility

Do you want a room full of paper clips? Probably not. If I switched the word paper clips for money, your answer would have changed because money has utility. Provide utility to others, and the money will come.

You may think you want money, but what you really want is what money represents to you. You may be able to exchange money for the things you want. So spend the time understanding what money means to you, and obtain what you want in the most efficient way possible.

Investing can be enjoyable and, at times, even exciting. If your investments provide utility to others, they are more likely to return money to you. J. Paul Getty's book, *How to Be Rich*, states that if you use your imagination and work hard to give people what they want, they will make you rich.

Reduce Spills by Cutting Unnecessary Expenses

If you work a job, determine your take-home pay after taxes. You can find this information by reviewing your tax documents or pay stubs. Review your bank and credit card statements to determine your necessary expenses. Your essential expenses include living costs such as rent or mortgage, transportation, food, clothing, utilities, and medical expenses. Think about whether there is any way you could reduce these expenses without sacrificing much. Add up the average cost of your necessary expenses. Subtract your essential expenses from your take-home pay. The result is the maximum amount you can save per month.

If you own a business, add any net income to the maximum amount you can save from the salary you pay yourself. According to the Pareto principle, roughly 80 percent of consequences come from 20 percent of causes, so you may have opportunities to cut costs and increase margins.[19] After adding investable cash flow and net income, you will have the maximum amount you can save.

Your cash flow may offer opportunities to save more. Consider the timing of necessary cash flows. If your cash flow needs are long-term, you may be able to earn substantial returns by investing the money in the meantime.

Analyze your luxuries. Look for unused subscriptions or recurring expenses that add little to your life. What habits could you easily spend less time on? (For example, for years, I made my lunch at home and walked a block to find cheaper parking when I went to the office.) Then subtract luxury expenses with little utility from your maximum potential savings to determine what you could reasonably save. Focus on ways to increase your income or reduce your expenses until you can save at least 10 percent of your income; the greater the percentage, the faster you will achieve financial freedom.

Save and Invest Automatically

Now that you know how much you can reasonably save, make saving an easy habit by automating it. Pay yourself before you spend. Have a portion of your check automatically transferred to your savings or brokerage account. If your employer offers direct deposit, have a portion of your paycheck automatically deposited into a checking account, and then transfer the funds to a savings, brokerage, or retirement account. Your bank and/or brokerage likely offers the ability to set up regular automatic transfers from your checking account to your

19. "Pareto Principle," *Wikipedia*, https://en.wikipedia.org/wiki/Pareto_principle.

savings or brokerage account. Transfer the funds to an account that is harder to access than your checking account so that you only withdraw funds when necessary. Finally, look for more ways to cut expenses or increase your income so you can save more each month.

There are many ways to automate investing, and you don't necessarily need a computer. Automating parts of investing takes you out of the decision-making process, which can be a good thing. You don't need to make every decision, and you probably shouldn't.

If you plan to hold funds for the long term, consider automating the timing of purchases with dollar cost averaging. For example, every other week, I purchased the maximum that the SEC would match into various funds through the Thrift Savings Plan (TSP).[20] My biweekly investment came right out of my paycheck, and I never saw it. Dollar cost averaging involves making automatic monthly contributions to a stock mutual fund or ETF, eliminating the decision of when or at what price to buy. Over time, dollar cost averaging typically results in lower average purchase prices than trying to time purchases, since you automatically buy more shares at lower prices.

For many securities, you may want to automate the sales decision by using trailing stops or stop orders. A market order immediately executes at the best available market price. This can be risky if you issue a large order relative to the stock's trading volume. A limit order specifies a price you are willing to accept and will only execute if the market reaches that price. A stop order is an order that triggers and becomes either your choice of a market order or a limit order when the current price reaches a specified price that you have chosen. A trailing stop order maintains a relationship with the market that you choose. For example, ten dollars below the current market price or 10 percent below the market price. This helps reduce your risk of a dramatic decline when you are not watching the market; however, market prices can drop so fast that it can be ineffective. Trailing stop-loss orders are excellent tools for locking in profits when you think a stock

20. *Thrift Savings Plan,* https://www.tsp.gov/.

could keep going much higher. The trailing stop order set 10 percent below your purchase price increases as the stock sets new highs. For example, setting a trailing stop at 10 percent below the ten-dollar market price means that if the bid drops to nine dollars, your broker will sell your position. However, if the stock goes to twenty dollars, your broker is authorized to sell at eighteen dollars. Primarily, trailing stop orders are effective with high-performing, highly liquid stocks that are gradually trending upward; in these instances, a little patience and a trailing stop order might make you a lot of money.

Algorithmic trading is synonymous with automated trading, but let's differentiate between fully automated trading and solving specific problems, such as when to buy particular investments. According to Britannica, algorithms are "systematic procedures that produce … the answer to a question or the solution of a problem."[21] You can and should automate many of the mundane tasks associated with investing. You should automate investment searches, whether you invest in stocks or real estate. Furthermore, you can automate many aspects of your analysis.

Fully automated trading would allow the computer to make all decisions; however, this may be very risky. Fully automated systems have the potential for making errors in logic and lacking common sense. If you fully automate a trading system, set up a separate corporation to hold the investments. In this way, if algorithmic trading goes bust, you may not.

Be Efficient

My grandfather's consulting business helped manufacturers become more efficient. As I understand it, my grandfather visited factories and thought creatively about how to reorganize them to reduce costs and increase productivity. So let us imagine that your life is like a factory where you produce a product or service. How can you make your factory more efficient? Let me share some principles that have worked in my own life. First, create a list of tasks to accomplish within a given time period or goal.

---

21. "Algorithm," *Britannica*, https://www.britannica.com/science/algorithm.

Task	Location	Deadline
Groceries	Ralph's	Tomorrow
Gas	Costco	Tomorrow
Client meeting	Flexible	Flexible
Drop kids off	School	8:30 a.m.
Pick the kids up	School	3:00 p.m.
Work project	Flexible	Tomorrow
Client meeting	Flexible	11:00 a.m.

Second, place tasks close in proximity on your schedule, reducing transportation costs or time. Finally, try scheduling events by priority or proximity. For example, by using the schedule above, we could save twenty-two minutes by getting gas at a local gas station and scheduling client meetings and our work project at the exact location. This small action of saving just twenty-two minutes a day works out to ninety-two hours over a year.

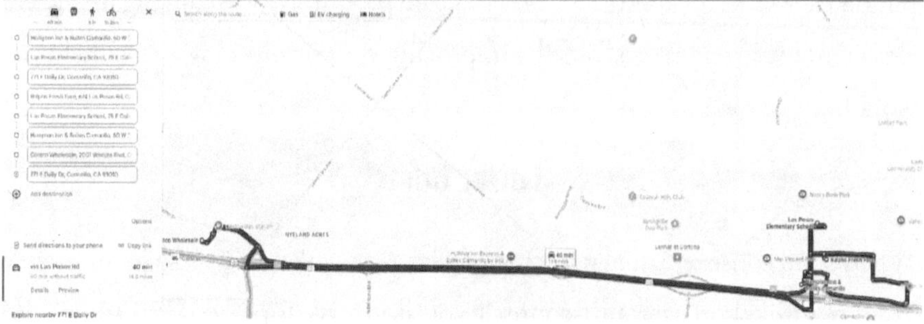

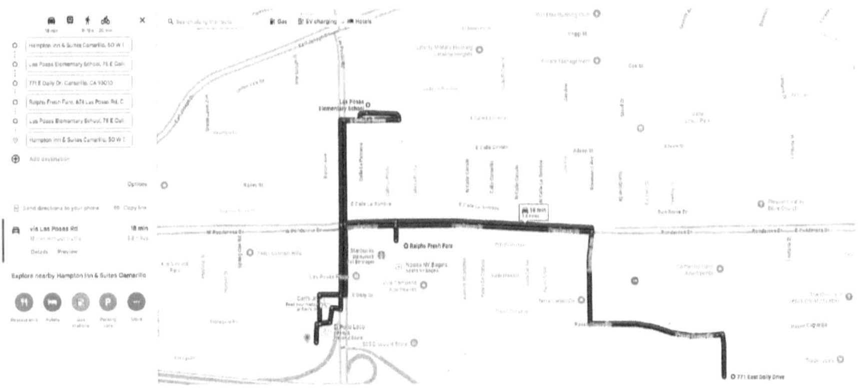

Creatively analyze tasks that routinely cost you considerable time or money. These are the tasks that may be worth automating. Investing additional time up front to develop or utilize technology could significantly reduce or even eliminate the task. Additionally, you could reduce costs and invested time by eliminating repetitive actions. Reduce, reuse, or recycle (RRR) at every opportunity. Applying this concept to many areas of your life may make you tremendously more efficient.

Furthermore, an ounce of prevention is worth a pound of cure. Don't delay; easily solvable problems can worsen if left to fester. In real estate, deferred maintenance over an extended period may leave a property in such poor condition that it becomes a major fixer-upper and may be hard to sell. Therefore, if the ramifications are potentially serious, address the problem while it's small and manageable.

Finally, increasing productivity may spread your costs, especially on large-volume tasks or products.

To recap: Create to-do lists, map out the tasks, reduce, reuse, recycle, don't put off easy tasks for tomorrow, and increase productivity. Reducing inefficiencies may reduce your costs, thereby improving your profits in whatever field you work in.

Lower Costs

When done consistently, negotiating better prices could save you a lot of money. You are unlikely to get a discount if you don't ask for one. I am sometimes surprised by the discounts I get when I ask. If you are shopping online, look for promotional codes. Retailers may not give a discount but may point you to a cheaper alternative that meets your needs. On the other hand, a private seller may anticipate you asking for a lower price.

Buying used may also save you a tremendous amount of money, which you could use to save and invest. For example, a new car drops in value significantly as soon as you drive it off the lot. In the first three to five years, your new car may lose as much as 50 to 70 percent of its value. Why not let someone else pay for most of the vehicle?

Consider two car owners: One buys a new car every three years, and the other buys a used car after three years and runs the car into the ground after ten years. The new car buyer pays $100,000 for the new vehicle, owns it for three years, and sells it for $50,000; his average cost per year is $16,666. The used car buyer buys the same car for $50,000 and uses it for ten years, at an average cost of $5,000 per year. So the difference in yearly spending is $11,666. Consider just this one difference over fifty years of investing: the difference at an 11 percent return, without even accounting for the increasing costs of cars. The used car buyer would have an additional $19.4 million. Hard to believe, but true.

I have a good friend who worked as a research scientist and didn't make much money. She bought everything used except for her condo. She had the most beautiful and elegant house. If she didn't tell you, you would never know that she had decorated it with almost entirely used items. With the additional savings, she was able to support her two aging parents and help her siblings in her home country. Buying used may allow you to do more with less.

Credit Cards

It is easy to get into trouble with credit cards, but they can increase your profit when used responsibly. Responsibly using credit cards means paying them off without paying interest. You may receive low or even zero-interest offers. Try to use these offers only if you can pay them off within the offer period with your income, unless you earn much more from your endeavors and it's the lowest interest available. Generally, paying off your credit cards monthly lets you use other people's money for a month without paying interest.

Many credit cards offer lucrative bonuses, such as points or cash back, to new and existing cardholders. You can use points in exchange for services or products. Credit cards can rebate you a percentage in cash or directly into an account. Rebate credit cards increase your bottom line when paid monthly. Use rebate cards for everything unless you receive a cash discount that is larger than your rebate, and always pay the entire balance monthly.

Generally, you should pay off consumer debt and debt on non-income-producing assets (such as clothes, cars, or boats). Many people fall into the trap of using credit cards to buy consumer goods or non-income-producing assets. This is why credit cards have such a bad reputation. If you've accumulated debt to purchase anything that does not appreciate or produce income, stop and pay off those debts. Make extra payments, or even better, pay high-interest-rate loans with a low-interest-rate consolidation loan or a second mortgage, then make additional payments to the new, lower-interest-rate loan.

Some credit cards may allow you to pay off other credit cards without interest for short periods. This was the perilous road that ultimately led to my bankruptcy many years ago. You will eventually need real income to pay off the credit cards, and if you cannot pay them off before they accumulate high interest rates, they may become difficult to pay off. So learn from my bad example what not to do.

Increasing Your Credit Scores[22,23]

Having high credit scores could save you hundreds of thousands of dollars over your lifetime. Different countries use different scoring systems or different

22. True Tamplin, "How to Improve Your Credit Score: 8 Simple Rules and Strategies," *Forbes*, https://www.forbes.com/sites/truetamplin/2024/11/28/how-to-improve-your-credit-score--8-simple-rules-and-strategies/.
23. Mikey Rox, "7 Easy Ways to Raise Your Credit Score This Year," https://www.wisebread.com/7-easy-ways-to-raise-your-credit-score-this-year.

bureaus. Some do not use numerical credit scores at all. Generally, improving your credit scores will decrease the interest you pay because your loan will be less risky. Therefore, you will benefit from improving your credit wherever you live, but the following pertains specifically to US credit bureaus.

In the US, your credit scores may be the price tag on your dreams. Your credit scores are numbers between 300 and 850. Although you can obtain a home loan with credit scores in the 500s, if your scores are below 670, you are paying higher rates on everything from car loans to home loans.[24] If your scores are 800 or higher, you have excellent credit and qualify for the best rates.

Raise your credit scores by 120 points, and you could save about 30 percent in interest. Bank of America's website provided an example where a $300,000 loan saved $91,000.[25]

Follow these steps to revolutionize your credit scores:

First, you need to know what you are working with. Head to https://www.annualcreditreport.com. This is your free, government-mandated peek behind the curtain. There is no credit card required, and no hidden fees. This is your credit score reconnaissance mission. Look for three things: errors, forgotten accounts, and other surprises.

Your payment history accounts for more than one third of your credit scores. Every single bill, every single month, either builds or destroys your financial reputation.

From today forward, pay everything on time. Set up automatic payments, if necessary. Use calendar reminders. Do whatever it takes. Because those scars take seven years to fully heal.

Credit utilization can boost your scores in just thirty days. If you have a $2,000 credit limit and you're carrying a $800 balance, you are at 40 percent utilization. You want to be under 30 percent. Generally, creditors want to see that you are not borrowing to the limit, because it means you could borrow more if you got

24. "FHA Loan Limits for 2025," *Experian*, https://www.experian.com/blogs/ask-experian/fha-loan-limits.
25. "How Credit Scores Affect Your Mortgage Rate," *Bank of America*, https://bettermoneyhabits.bankofamerica.com/en/home-ownership/how-credit-affects-mortgage-rate.

into trouble, and it reduces their risk in the short term. As your debt increases, so does your risk. It makes sense, right?

If you ask your credit card company for a limit increase, say from $2,000 to $4,000, suddenly $800 becomes 20 percent utilization instead of 40 percent. Your scores may jump as a result. Your credit mix shows lenders that you're good with all sorts of credit. But here's the key: Don't go crazy. Build this diversity over time.

People think opening five credit cards in two months will boost their scores. This triggers what lenders call credit-seeking behavior, and they think you are desperate. Instead, space out your credit applications (for example: one new account every six months). Your credit scores reward patience, not impulsiveness.

Dispute every single error through the credit bureaus. Write letters, make calls, and document everything. The law is on your side here. Credit bureaus must resolve or remove disputes within thirty days.

Your oldest account is the one that anchors your credit history. Close it, and you will shorten your average account age, which can hurt your scores. Keep that old card active by making a small purchase every few months.

Finally, sign up for credit monitoring. Check your scores monthly and your full report quarterly. Additionally, consider freezing your credit through these services. This can help protect you from identity theft. The sooner you identify problems, the easier they are to resolve.

Improving your credit scores can lead to a better life. Obtain lower interest rates, insurance premiums, better apartment options, and even job opportunities. Every additional point to your credit scores may yield dividends for decades.

Your credit scores are a powerful tool in your financial arsenal, and now you have the blueprint to master it. The question is not whether you can improve your credit scores—you absolutely can. The question is: Will you?

Start today. Take control of your financial destiny. Good credit is not luck; it is strategy. And now you have the strategy!

Purchase Your Primary Residence

Once you have decent credit, save 5 percent of a home's purchase price in a stable or growing area plus a safety net of six months or more; then start looking for real estate. The idea behind purchasing your first property is to reduce or even eliminate your living expenses, saving the difference and thereby accelerating your path to financial freedom. For example, you buy a four-unit building with the 5 percent down payment you saved using Federal Housing Administration (FHA) financing (3.5 percent down and 1.5 percent closing costs).[26] If the rent from the other three units covers the building's expenses, you live for free and can invest the money you would usually pay in rent, mortgage, maintenance, etc. This idea alone could accelerate your path to financial freedom by many years, enabling you to save 30 percent or more of your income.

Purchasing your first home, condo, or multiunit property can be exciting and a little scary. It felt like such a huge commitment the first time, but I should have done it much earlier. Even if you won't live in the same area forever, buying may make sense. Later, you can always sell or rent the house; however, you ideally need to hold it for more than five to ten years.

Purchasing your home can help stabilize your living expenses. In the long term, buying has generally made sense over renting in terms of quality of life, total outlay, and appreciation. Continuing to save may reduce your payment by eliminating additional fees on low-down-payment loans; however, waiting comes with the risk that housing will appreciate by more than you saved. Opportunities arise in which it may be cheaper to buy than rent. If the market currently provides you with a chance like this, don't hesitate; they don't usually last long.

Your house may even provide you with an income source. Having roommates can be enjoyable, and renting a room or two may help you pay the mortgage. Alternatively, buildings with four units or fewer qualify for the same financing as regular homes, so you can live for free with the right small rental property. Finally, you could turn the property into a short-term or long-term rental when

26. *US Department of Housing and Urban Development*, https://www.hud.gov/fha.

you move. Repeatedly buying properties, moving in, and renting them out may help you secure better interest rates, gain more leverage, or make lower down payments. This can also accelerate your financial freedom.

Reducing Your Housing Costs

The average person spends more on living expenses than on any other expense, so many may have opportunities to cut spending and save more.

If purchasing is too expensive now, renting may be your best option. When I rented, I always tried to get by with the smallest apartment that met my needs. Sometimes, it felt like a huge sacrifice, but it enabled me to save faster than I could have otherwise. If you're single, consider renting a room in a house. If the rental has extra rooms, get a roommate. You may be able to relocate to an adjacent area that is cheaper. If relatives are willing to help you out, living with them could significantly increase your monthly savings until you can buy property.

If you already own your home, increase your income by thinking creatively. You could rent living space. Alternatively, consider how unique your property is and if there is anything people might pay to use. For example, if you own a house on the edge of a major highway, someone might pay you to put up a sign on your property facing the highway. Alternatively, a house near a major entertainment venue might present the opportunity to rent parking spaces.

When you own a home, your expenses fall into several major categories: financing, taxes, maintenance, and insurance. When your mortgage is nearly fully amortized, paying off your loan may make sense since you cannot deduct much interest, but the payment could be large. Refinancing may make sense if your current loan has a high interest rate. If prices have dropped, the county may reduce your taxes if you ask for a reassessment. You always have the option to defer maintenance, but this is a bad choice in the long term. Instead, shop around for the cheapest skilled contractor. If you are handy, consider doing maintenance yourself. Finally, shop around for high-rated insurance companies with inexpensive insurance rates. You can also raise your deductible, especially if you would not make a small claim anyway.

Check Your Knowledge

1. What are ways to increase your savings?

2. Describe how you can automatically save and invest.

3. What are some ways to become more efficient?

Chapter Summary/Key Takeaways

Remember the bucket that overflowed? Financial freedom often comes from finding a balance between increasing income and managing expenses. Exploring ways to provide value to others can open new opportunities, and many people find that creating a budget and automating savings helps them stay on track.

CHAPTER FOUR:

Take Time

All we have to decide is what to do with the time that is given us.
—*J. R. R. Tolkien,* The Fellowship of the Ring

Warren Buffett's life demonstrates what is possible, given enough time. Warren Buffett, the "oracle of Omaha," was born in 1930 and developed an interest in business as early as seven years old. Reportedly, his favorite book as a child was *One Thousand Ways to Make $1,000.*[27] Mr. Buffett bought his first stock at age eleven. When he was in high school, he wanted to be a stockbroker and did not want to go to college; however, his father insisted he attend college. He enrolled at Columbia Business School after learning that Benjamin Graham taught there. Benjamin Graham wrote one of the best books on value investing, *The Intelligent Investor.* Mr. Buffett learned value investing from Benjamin Graham and is reportedly the only student ever to receive an A+ from Graham. Mr. Buffett likes to say that he got rich slowly, like a snowball that builds into a giant avalanche.

After college, he worked for Graham as a securities analyst for a few years before eventually starting his own business, the Buffett Partnership, Ltd. From 1956 through 1969, Buffett ran the Buffett Partnership, earning a 31.6 percent annual return with no losing years, compared to 9.1 percent for the Dow Jones Industrial Average. In 1969, he dissolved the partnership and transferred all of the

27. F. C. Minaker, *One Thousand Ways to Make $1,000* (1936).

assets to Berkshire Hathaway, one of the partnership's holdings. Since converting the partnership to Berkshire Hathaway, Mr. Buffett continued his stellar performance. As of February 2020, he outperformed the S&P 500 in thirty-seven of fifty-five years. If you had invested $1,000 in Berkshire Hathaway in 1965, you would have had $27 million in February 2020.[28]

As of January 2026, Mr. Buffett retired, and two news sources reported his net worth at $148 billion, making him the ninth richest person in the world, and that's after he donated $208 billion to various foundations.[29] Mr. Buffett set an admirable example not just as an investor but as a philanthropist and a human being. His extreme example resulted from high average returns compounded over a long time. According to Mr. Buffett, "Time is your friend." He made 99 percent of his net worth after age fifty; not because he suddenly got smarter, but because compounding finally had enough *time to have exponential results.*

Time Ignites STAR

For years, bamboo seeds sit underground, and people see nothing; then, the bamboo shoots up *ninety feet in six weeks.* The growth isn't magic. The *time* spent building roots make the explosion possible. *Compounding works the same way, so invest for the long term.*

Time is the exponential component of the STAR method and the future value formula, and it's the most essential element if you want to build massive wealth. Having an extended time period increases the likelihood that your assets and savings will grow exponentially, depending on your average returns.

Time is a measurement of change represented by a quantity of periods. We invented time to measure the periods of our lives. In our financial lives, we care about two time periods: compounding frequency and time horizon.

28. Al Root, "Breaking Down the Buffet Formula: Berkshire Hathaway's Returns by the Numbers," *Barron's*, February 25, 2020, https://www.barrons.com/articles/berkshire-hathaways-investing-returns-a-breakdown-by-numbers-51582633800.
29. "Warren Buffett," *Wikipedia*, https://en.wikipedia.org/wiki/Warren_Buffett?utm_source=copilot.com.

Compounding Frequency

Compounding frequency refers to the number of times we add interest to the principal each year. Annual compounding means we compound just once per year. Semiannual compounding means we add interest twice, with a smaller amount applied biannually. Compounding can occur monthly, weekly, daily, or continuously. Each time we earn a return, it becomes part of the principal. Compounding more frequently may lead to higher annualized returns.

Time Horizon

The time horizon is the total number of years needed to reach your goals, or the time until you need your money back. Compounding is what causes money to grow into enormous amounts over time. To take full advantage of compounding, investments must compound for many periods. The more years you have, the harder your money can work for you. The longer the time horizon, the longer compounding must work, and the more aggressive you can be. If you can expand your time horizon, you can achieve loftier goals more easily.

Total Time Periods

The total time periods are the result of the compounding frequency multiplied by the investment horizon in years. Together, they are the exponential piece of compound interest. Increasing the compounding frequency increases the annual return, and increasing the time horizon increases the future value. You want to maximize time periods by increasing either your time horizon, compounding periods, or both.

Let's consider two simple changes early in your career and how they could affect your retirement. Let's say you found free parking a block farther from work instead of paying fifteen dollars to park under your office, and/or you made one less trip to Starbucks, saving an additional five dollars during the day (I used to make several coffee trips on particularly rough days). How could those changes affect your retirement in general? Furthermore, if you left that money in a checking account and invested it at the end of the year rather than weekly, would that make a difference?

Over the past forty years, the average return for the S&P 500 was approximately 11.5 percent (including dividends), and returns were positively skewed. Let's imagine that sometime during this period, three young entrepreneurs had the opportunity to invest in an S&P 500 index fund. The first entrepreneur paid for the parking and the extra Starbucks run. Since they never invested, they had nothing to show for the added expenses when they retired. The second innovative entrepreneur set up a Keogh plan (similar to a pension or individual retirement account ("IRA") for entrepreneurs), accumulated an additional $20 a day in their checking account, and then invested $7,300 in a Keogh plan each year for forty years. As a result, the second investor had an additional $496,000 at twenty years, which grew to $4.8 million at forty years when they were ready to retire. Finally, our last knowledgeable entrepreneur made a weekly contribution of $140 to their Keogh plan; this intelligent investor accumulated $566,000 in twenty years, which grew to $6.2 million in total by the time they retired.

The Magic of Compounding

The magic of compounding returns is the biggest
mathematical discovery of all time.
—*Benjamin Graham*

Sometimes our minds are not reasonable in perceiving the potential of exponential growth. The ancient story of the invention of chess demonstrates how we may underestimate exponential growth. The inventor of chess presented the game to the emperor of India, who was so impressed that he offered the inventor any reward he desired. The inventor asked for one grain of rice on the first square of the chessboard, doubling the number of grains on each subsequent square until all sixty-four squares were filled. The emperor agreed to this modest request but soon realized his mistake. The payment was eighteen quintillion grains of rice, or more than all the grain in the world. The number eighteen quintillion is so large that it's a little hard to perceive, but it is equivalent to one billion multiplied by eighteen billion. You also likely underestimate what is possible with enough time periods and positive returns.[30]

The simple recipe for achieving exponential future wealth combines time with positive returns. There are ways to reduce the likelihood of going astray. First, understanding what is possible may keep you focused on the potential rather than setbacks. Your strategy should be scalable and flexible. Automating tasks will make investing effortless. Finally, we will discuss methods for managing risks.

The Rule of Seventy-Two

The rule of seventy-two estimates how quickly your wealth will grow. If you divide seventy-two by your average annual return, you will get the approximate number of years it will take your investment to double. For example, if you divide seventy-two by a 24 percent rate of return, you will get three, so your wealth doubles approximately every three years. At 12 percent, your wealth will double in approximately six years. At 7.2 percent, your wealth will double in about ten years. In twenty-one years, an investor with 24 percent returns would increase his wealth ninety-one times, but an investor with 7.2 percent returns would have quadrupled his wealth. High returns and many periods will result in exponential growth.

To increase future exponential results, you would need to add years, returns, and/or compounding periods. Investing more frequently and delaying retirement are two simple ways to increase compounding. You can influence or control your investment horizon, compounding periods, and returns to a certain extent. Exponential results will follow but will present challenges.

Scalability and Flexibility

Small investors can implement strategies that offer potentially significant returns that large institutions may not be able to due to their size. For example, companies with lesser amounts of stock outstanding (i.e., microcap stocks) might offer

30. "Wheat and chessboard problem," *Wikipedia*, https://en.wikipedia.org/wiki/Wheat_and_chessboard_problem.

higher returns, but because they have small capitalizations, a large institution could not buy them without reducing their returns, as doing so would drive up the price. Furthermore, since the large institution would have to purchase many different microcaps, it would know less and less about the investments as it added more. On the other hand, a small investor would not affect market prices. Learning to invest and developing expertise in scalable investment areas are preferable. You must be flexible if your ideas are not scalable.

Emotional Control and Discipline

Having emotional control and discipline is essential for a successful investor. As the amount of money you invest increases, you will likely be more emotional about your decisions; therefore, it's important to develop emotional control. Discipline will help ensure consistent results.

Having emotional control helps you make rational, generally better decisions. Recognize how you feel when making decisions. One technique to avoid making decision emotionally is to make them after the markets close. Other ways to develop emotional control include delaying decisions until you have calmed down, taking a deep breath, or practicing meditation. Learning to meditate can make you a better investor. Use Benjamin Franklin's approach to decision-making by making a list of the pros and cons, reflecting on them, and making your decision.

Having discipline means obeying your preset rules. Unless you have good reasons, you should stick to your established investing rules and risk management principles, regardless of the outcome, good or bad. Automating processes reduces required discipline. This takes you out of decisions entirely. Preestablish rules to guide your decision-making. Set specific purchase criteria, such as a checklist, to objectively determine whether to invest. Establish risk management rules. Having discipline and investing in checklists and risk management rules will help you stay on track and even profit substantially when markets go wild.

The more barriers there are to withdraw funds or liquidate an investment (e.g., tax penalties for IRAs, or buyers' markets in real estate), the less emotional control or discipline you will need. Costs or hassles can keep you invested even when you might normally panic and sell. For long-term investments, barriers to accessing funds or liquidating assets may be a good thing because selling when prices are down generally reduces your returns.

The Importance of Cash Flow

Cash flow makes volatility and uncertainty bearable. Cash flow is the lifeblood of a business. For investors, passive income or cash flow enables you to live through volatility without selling at low prices.

When it was time to sell my first house, the market had declined so much that I would have lost my entire equity after paying the selling commissions. I realized the market rent would cover all my property-related expenses, so I decided to rent the property rather than sell it. When the market recovered, I pulled my equity out by refinancing, and the property continues to pay for itself. The fact that I was not paying the mortgage and other related expenses enabled me to hold on to the property and eventually made it a sound investment.

Liquidity

Liquidity is essential when you don't have sufficient cash flow or when you want to sell. The most liquid market is the market with the most buyers and sellers. In a liquid market, transactions usually occur quickly with little price change. Having a mixture of liquid and illiquid investments is generally a promising idea. For example, stocks and bonds of popular companies, or open-ended no-load mutual funds, are usually very liquid.

Illiquid investments can offer higher returns; however, their prices fluctuate more wildly. If an investor needs cash quickly, they may need to sell at a deeply discounted price. Illiquid investments can become very liquid if demand is high. For example, real estate is not very liquid; therefore, always keep enough liquid assets to prevent a distressed sale. The real estate market is cyclical and will eventually return to a seller's market.

Check Your Knowledge

1. What are the components of total time periods, and how are they combined?
2. Why do total time periods have such a powerful effect on future investment values?
3. How can you increase your emotional control as your portfolio gets larger?
4. Explain the importance of cash flow in achieving exponential results.
5. Explain why it is essential to balance liquid and illiquid investments.

Chapter Summary/Key Takeaways

Increasing the total number of periods could dramatically improve your results. Compound frequency refers to the number of compounding periods in a year. The time horizon is the period required to reach your goal. You can add either the compounding frequency or the time horizon to improve your results, because the total periods are the product of the two. Finally, we discussed the following ways to achieve exponential results without going bankrupt:

- Focus on long-term potential. Understand what is possible eventually, so believe in your future.
- Be flexible.
- Develop emotional control and discipline.
- Limit leverage to the debt supported by the investment's cash flow.
- Strike a reasonable balance between liquid and illiquid investments so that you do not put yourself in a distressed situation.

CHAPTER FIVE:

Add or Reallocate Assets

The best time to plant a tree was twenty years ago. The second-best time is now.
—Chinese proverb

Robert T. Kiyosaki is a self-made multimillionaire who has authored many books. Still, I consider two of them to be particularly excellent because they really opened my mind to a unique way of thinking about assets. Those two books are *Rich Dad Poor Dad* and *Rich Dad's Cashflow Quadrant.* Although I had read other books that said similar things, these two books really showed me how wealthy people think about assets. Basically, Mr. Kiyosaki explained that your assets generate cash flow for you, and your liabilities require you to pay money.

If you have not read Mr. Kiyosaki's books, I highly recommend them. His personal style and profound content might change your life. Analysts use a similar approach to value assets.

Financial analysts measure value by the amount of future cash flow an asset generates now and is expected to generate in the future. You should not pay more for an investment than you can recover with an acceptable return. So you want to maximize the yield and growth of your assets. If you optimize yield and growth, your resale values will increase. Add productive assets that maximize cash flow and drive growth; these characteristics will help you achieve financial freedom.

Choose: Burdened or Liberated?

The purpose of this chapter is to demonstrate how to shift from assets that trap you to assets that free you. Sell assets that cost you money, like expensive cars, boats, collectibles, or overly concentrated positions. Buy productive assets that reduce expenses or offer exceptional growth and cash yield.

Assets Versus Liabilities

Owning lots of assets may not lead to financial freedom. Many assets require you to pay money to keep them, such as storage or maintenance costs; they are like shiny shackles. They may look attractive, but they keep you trapped. If used infrequently, leasing these types of assets temporarily may be smarter.

Some assets may not generate cash flow but may save you money over time (for example, owning your residence). You want to own, but these assets are unlikely to make you rich on their own.

Productive assets generate value for others through what they produce or provide, and they generate cash flow for their owners too. Your goal should be to own as many productive assets as possible.

Liabilities, on the other hand, create obligations to pay money; think of them as negative assets because they reduce your equity (i.e., the amount that is yours and not owed to someone else). Liability examples include loans and bills. For our purposes, liabilities require payments.

Are cars and boats assets or liabilities? Technically, they are assets because you can sell them for cash; however, their value decreases over time, potentially rendering them worthless. Since you must store and maintain them, they are luxury leashes. You want to own assets that will generate more money than you paid for them. Owning assets that require maintenance and whose values are declining will make it harder for you to achieve financial freedom.

So how can you increase your assets and reduce your liabilities? First, you need to assess your assets. Think objectively about whether what you own is generating value to others or will generate more if held. If not, consider selling some assets, paying off your most expensive loans, or buying another asset with better cash flow. You should aim to own undervalued, cash flow-producing, and appreciating assets (i.e., assets that increase in value). Especially when used infrequently, consider leasing items that do not meet these criteria (for example, boats, planes, cars, equipment, etc.).

If you are early in your career and do not have wealthy parents, you probably have few assets to speak of. If you want to accelerate your journey to financial freedom, then using other people's money is one way to do so.

Other People's Money: The Various Forms of Leverage

Give me a lever long enough and a fulcrum on which to place it, and I shall move the world.

—Archimedes of Syracuse, Greece

When used diligently, financial leverage could enable you to move the world and may significantly accelerate your path to financial freedom. Other people's money encompasses various forms of leverage such as borrowing, raising capital, or float. Other people's money may allow you to do things you could not do alone. Even if you have money to invest, other people's money may increase your returns by giving you leverage.[31]

Some examples of other people's money include loans, equity, and float. If you buy a home or rentals, you will likely use other people's money when you get a loan. If you start a small business, you may raise capital from friends or family, or maybe even strangers later on. Finally, float is money you hold that you owe to someone else, but it is not yet due. For example, you are using float when you charge a credit card before the payment due date, even though no interest is accumulating. So you may be using other people's money without realizing it. When used effectively, creatively, and honestly, other people's money provides the opportunity for great wealth through leverage but carries responsibilities to

31. Keep in mind that with leverage comes additional risk. Increasing possible returns also increases losses if prices move against you.

the investors who gave you the money. Here are the stories of three men who used other people's money to become billionaires.

Borrowing

Daniel Ludwig's life story provides an example of what is possible. Mr. Ludwig started out with nothing and received little formal education, yet his wealth grew to an estimated $4.5 billion. Born in South Haven, Michigan, in 1897, he dropped out of school in the eighth grade, so he did not complete high school. He started his first business at nineteen years old by borrowing $5,000. He then used the $5,000 to buy and refurbish a boat that had allegedly been used to ship rum during Prohibition.[32]

In the 1930s, Mr. Ludwig began building tankers, funding construction costs by prearranging charters and using them as collateral for deferred bank loans. Banks deferred the loans until the charter's contract began. As Mr. Ludwig paid off loans, he acquired new ships with minimal capital investment, thereby continually improving his cash flow.

In 1936, Mr. Ludwig founded National Bulk Carriers, which owned and operated oil tankers and bulk carriers. Eventually, he became one of the largest multinationals in the world, with assets of several billion dollars. During World War II, he owned and operated welding shipyards that built tankers for National Bulk Carriers, which supported the US's war efforts.

In 1952, Mr. Ludwig invented the oil supertanker. Although known as a global shipping magnate, he diversified into hotels, refineries, salt and coal mines, and citrus farms. At its peak, Mr. Ludwig's empire spanned two hundred companies in fifty countries, and he employed more than twenty thousand people. In 1982, Mr. Ludwig was the wealthiest man in the United States, according to the *Forbes* 400 list.

---

32. "Business: Twilight of a Tycoon," *TIME*, November 30, 1970, https://content.time.com/time/subscriber/article/0,33009,904563-1,00.html.

Raising Capital

Steve Jobs founded Apple with his friend Steve Wozniak in 1976. They met at the Homebrew Computer Club and decided to build their computer, the Apple I, using parts they bought or borrowed. Mr. Jobs and Mr. Wozniak produced and sold approximately two hundred Apple I computers to computer stores and enthusiasts at prices ranging from $475 to $666.66.[33]

Before its initial public offering (IPO), Apple raised $230,000 in initial seed equity capital. On December 12, 1980, the company offered 4.6 million shares at $22 per share, raising $101 million in its IPO. Investors oversubscribed (i.e., demand for the stock exceeded the number of shares sold publicly), and Apple's IPO and the stock price rose to $29 on the first trading day. Apple's market capitalization (the value of its equity) was $1.778 billion at the end of the first day. As of December 2025, Apple had a market capitalization of $4 trillion.[34]

Mr. Jobs proved to be a creative genius by inventing products such as the Apple II, the Macintosh, Pixar, Next, the Cube, the iPhone, the iPad, and the iPod. However, he may never have had the opportunity to show the world the extent of his creative genius without the initial equity he'd raised from investors.

Float [35,36]

Warren Buffett used insurance float as leverage to supercharge his investment returns by investing the money he collected from premiums before paying out claims. Insurance float is the difference between the premiums an insurance company receives and the claims it pays. Insurance float is a loan from policyholders that an insurance company can use to invest until a benefits claim. Float has enabled Mr. Buffett's company, Berkshire Hathaway, to use leverage.

Through underwriting profits and value investing, Mr. Buffett used long-term

33. "Apple I," *Wikipedia*, May 2023.
34. "Apple - Funding, Financials, Valuation & Investors," *Crunchbase*, May 2023.
35. Dave Ahern, "Float: How Insurance Companies Can Leverage Buffett's Secret to Wealth," *Sather Research*, September 30, 2019, https://einvestingforbeginners.com/insurance-float-ahern/.
36. Dillon Jacobs, "The Insurance Float: the Secret Behind Warren Buffett's Wealth," *FinMasters*, April 29, 2025, https://finmasters.com/warren-buffett-insurance-float/.

float as leverage to generate high returns over time using a disciplined approach. He generated an underwriting profit by collecting premiums that exceeded the claims and expenses he paid. The genius of this is that while you or I would pay interest to borrow from a bank to invest long-term, Mr. Buffett earned a profit to use float as leverage to invest.

From 1967 through 2024, Mr. Buffett's insurance float grew from $16 million to an estimated $171 billion, based on public filings. He used the float to invest in consumer monopolies such as Coca-Cola and Apple, and to purchase entire companies such as Geico. During the same period, Berkshire Hathaway has grown its book and market value at a compounded rate of about twice that of the S&P 500.

I am not suggesting that you buy an insurance company to obtain a source of float, but rather that float in any form can be a source of tremendous free leverage. Most of us have access to some float, which is an asset entrusted to you before you need to pay it out. Here are a few examples:

1. When you use a credit card that offers a rebate of, say, 2 percent, and you receive thirty days of float every month
2. The interest and penalty-free window after taxes are owed but before they are paid
3. The days between payroll processing and payday

If this money earns some low-risk interest, these sources of short-term float could turn an unprofitable business into a very profitable one.

Price Versus Value

Price is the amount you pay, but intrinsic value is what you get. Stock prices may fluctuate significantly as supply and demand fluctuate. A company's intrinsic value is what it's worth. Intrinsic value is the value an analyst would assign to it. It is the present value of expected future cash flows (i.e., everything you will receive from owning the asset in the future). Value estimates may be highly subjective due to uncertainty or differing opinions; for example, such differences are one reason stock prices fluctuate wildly. Prices may be too high or too low, but they tend to move toward their intrinsic value over time. As the expected cash flow increases, so does the inherent value, and vice versa.

For example, let's imagine that I pay a low price to acquire a profitable software company with a new service that everyone wants. The CEO is a hardworking, genius programmer. As sales increase, so does cash flow and the intrinsic value of the company. Buying an asset with an increasing intrinsic value will increase the likelihood that you may sell it for a profit in the end.

As another example, let's say I pay a lot for a pay phone company with strong historical cash flow. Mobile phones reduce demand for my product, which decreases cash flow; eventually, the company goes out of business, and I lose my investment.

So sell overvalued assets with decreasing cash flows and buy undervalued assets with increasing cash flows. Create a watch list of investments you want to buy based on your expectations. Then, only buy assets that are priced low or fairly.

The concepts of price and value apply to real estate, too. When you buy a house, you get an appraisal because the bank will not lend you more than they think the property is worth. The bank wants some protection. Benjamin Graham would have called that a margin of safety. The concept of intrinsic value is important because it helps to ensure that your investments have a margin of safety. Admitting that values are subjective, we can think more clearly about prices and the sources of opportunity to buy undervalued assets.

You can even apply the concept of price and value to yourself, so let's get introspective for a minute. Have you ever paid a fair amount for a product or service and still felt like it was a good deal because the value was higher than what you paid? If value is what you get, it makes sense that you feel happy if you think you received more than what you paid. If you provide an excellent value to your customers, even if you charge a lot, they will likely feel good and will come back. What more can we provide to our customers, employers, etc.? The customer may come back and buy more. Your employer may give you that raise. By providing an excellent value to others, you will profit.

Expertise may reveal opportunities and allow us to provide value to others. By specializing, you may see what others do not. For example, if you are a customer, you may recognize that a product is extraordinary before the general market comes to the same conclusion. You develop product expertise by researching alternatives. Expertise is knowledge, and knowledge can give you the confidence to act in the right conditions. In addition, the services you provide to others will be valuable. Value generates opportunity and preserves wealth. As discussed, low prices relating to value offer an opportunity for profit and protection.

A crisis can lead to an extreme opportunity. To recognize a situation, you need to be aware of current events. You must be present and alert to your surroundings. During crises, prices are artificially low, and extreme opportunities may exist. When others are fearful or need liquidity, you may provide relief and liquidity. One problem is that when everyone is scared, you will likely be scared, too. You may recognize that prices are lower than intrinsic values but lack the courage to act. When opportunity presents itself, your expertise may give you the courage to act decisively.

So develop your expertise, deliver value, preserve your wealth, and be present. These are the keys to gaining extraordinary wealth.

Work Wealth Versus Monetary Wealth

Beyond the tangible items you own, your skills and your ability to work are intangible assets because they can generate value for others. I bring up work wealth here because it is an asset that is often overlooked when considering what you have. The stability of your work affects the amount of financial reserves you need. If you become unemployed regularly, you need liquidity to cover your expenses while you are unemployed. You should have savings that you can easily access to cover living expenses for at least six months, or longer if your unemployment could last longer.

When you're young, you can work for many years, so you have a lot of wealth in the form of your ability to work; however, you may have no monetary wealth. As you grow older and save, your financial wealth may increase, but your ability to work will decrease. At some point, many people find it challenging to work. Therefore, the balance between your work and your monetary wealth influences your ability to take risks. Additionally, the more time you have before you'll need the money, the more risk you can take. Therefore, you will want to think about setting up various buckets of wealth for different purposes, and then take appropriate risks for each one.

Your ability to take risks in your portfolio is directly proportional to how much time you have remaining until you'll need the money, how badly you need the money, and whether you have extra money. A wealth bucket that is intended for next year should be in a low-risk, low-volatility asset. Invest in very conservative assets when your goals are short-term, for necessities, and there is no surplus (i.e., when you do not have more money than you need to meet your goals). Consider high-return and high-risk assets for your long-term goals, for luxuries, and when you have a surplus.

Your Personal Balance Sheet

Your current personal balance sheet is a snapshot of all your assets and liabilities; it covers everything you own and owe. Your assets include anything that can generate value for people. A burning desire is priceless. Your knowledge, abilities, and work ethic may be your most valuable assets, although it is hard to put a value on them. Your liabilities are any obligations that require you to pay money.

Take an honest assessment of your life and holdings. List all your assets and liabilities. Do not stress over the amounts; this is just about awareness and observing where you are in life. Knowing where you are coming from is a crucial step in determining how to get where you want to go. Knowing what you must work with, you can adjust and plan how to achieve your goals.

Here is an example of what your personal balance sheet might look like early in your life. Notice that most of your assets comprise your ability to work and contribute to society. Additionally, you might have few physical assets. Even if you come from a wealthy family, you may be utterly dependent on the generosity of your family and the value of a few assets in your name.

Example Balance Sheet Early in Career	
Tangible Assets	**Amount**
Cash and securities	$500,000
Real estate	$1,000,000
Intangible Assets	
The present value of your working years	$10,000,000
The present value of copyrights, patents, etc.	$500,000
Total Assets	$ 12,000,000
Liabilities	
Present value of car notes	$50,000
Present value of mortgages	$ 200,000
Present value of taxes due	$ 40,000
Present value of living expenses	$ 10,000,000
Equity or Net Worth	$1,710,000
Total Liabilities and Equity	$12,000,000

Here is an example of what your personal balance sheet might look like after retirement. Notice that most of your assets shifted to cash, securities, real estate, and rights to things you created. You will not or cannot work. So it is essential to take more risks when you are young; later, income from your assets becomes more important after you retire.

Example Balance Sheet After Retirement	
Tangible Assets	**Amount**
Cash and securities	$4,000,000
Real estate	$10,000,000
Intangible Assets	
The present value of your working years	$ 0
The present value of copyrights, patents, etc.	$1,000,000
Total Assets	$15,000,000
Liabilities	
Present value of car notes	$0
Present value of mortgages	$ 0
Present value of taxes due	$ 100,000
Present value of living expenses	$500,000
Equity or Net Worth	$14,375,000
Total Liabilities and Equity	$ 15,000,000

The remainder of this chapter will guide you in using this balance sheet to shift from assets that require payment to assets that generate cash inflow. Simply put, sell things that cost you money and buy things that make you money. Additionally, shift away from expensive, low-yielding, or declining assets and purchase low-cost, high-yielding, or growing assets.

Intangible Assets

Increasing your income by getting a better job or improving your skills can build your intangible assets. Consider your likes and dislikes when identifying opportunities; then review job postings for your ideal careers and examine the required skills. If you are having difficulty identifying opportunities, consider taking a psychological profile, which may help you identify jobs that match your personality. For example, take the Strong Interest Inventory or the Myers

Briggs Type Indicator. Do not let these tests limit you. Only use them for ideas. You can and will evolve during your life. If you have a passion for something, go for it. The more you enjoy what you do, the easier it will be to work long hours. Imagine the person you will need to become. Then determine the skills required to do the work you want to do.

Anywhere and everywhere, learn the skills you need. Enroll in online training courses, college courses, company training, industry seminars, etc. Join professional associations. Find a mentor. Observe and talk with people who have different perspectives and experiences. Read white papers and case studies. Volunteer for new tasks or projects that will help you develop necessary skills.

On the other hand, if everybody needs a product or service but nobody wants to provide it, it may be very profitable. Consider needs in your area of expertise. If you can solve a problem, you may have an idea for an excellent product or service.

You can offer a service or product that people need or want. Look for opportunities to help local businesses. Alternatively, you could start a blog, podcast, YouTube channel, online store, tutoring service, pet-sitting business, photography service, etc. Are there platforms that could connect you with clients who need your skills? Expand and use your network to find opportunities for referrals. Invest in streams of passive income, such as rental properties, dividend stocks, or lending.

Selling is a skill worth developing, whether you're selling your own skills or your products. It doesn't matter how good your skills or products are; if you don't sell them, nobody will ever know.

Continually increase your income. If your income is less than twice your needs, it may be challenging to save and invest. The more income you have, the more you can save, which creates a self-reinforcing cycle. Whatever your work is, be the best you can be at that type of work. Success begets success. When you excel, it becomes a habit, and vice versa.

Surviving Storms

During storms, sometimes the best anyone can do is survive or lose as little real value as possible. Precious metals and other forms of high-value compact wealth are held not for what they earn but for what they preserve. Precious metals offer no yield, yet they embody a form of wealth that is dense and durable. They are usually indifferent to changes in governments or credit cycles. Historically, metals have served to preserve wealth during instability. These physical holdings play a role that is difficult to replicate.

Gold, in particular, is less an investment than a form of financial stillness. It tends to matter most in the rare chapters when institutions wobble and mobility becomes valuable. Although I have used gold as an example, other compact, high-value items (such as other precious metals or gems) could serve the same purpose. Today, investors can hold portable, high-value assets in many forms, including coins, physical bullion, gemstones, fine jewelry, watches, rare artifacts, miniature high-value art, or cryptocurrency cold wallets. You might classify these items as collectibles. I value precious metals relative to median housing prices; this gives me an objective means to determine whether the metal or housing is expensive in relative terms. These items do not contribute to your financial freedom but provide a type of insurance. Since collectibles function more like an insurance policy, it may be easy to end up owning too many.

Sell Physical Nonproductive Assets

In life, there will be detours, and some may be self-imposed. (For example, I was very tempted to buy a boat at one point.) It may be appealing to buy luxury goods like boats, high-end furniture, and top-of-the-line home electronics, but at the end of the day, they'll only delay your financial freedom. These are assets that don't produce a cash flow for you, so be extremely cautious with your purchases, and consider when it's time to sell them.

Understanding who values what you are selling most can help you effectively target your sales efforts. Different assets appeal to other types of buyers.

For instance, a classic car might attract car enthusiasts, a unique painting might attract art collectors, and a profitable business might attract competitors or investors.

Understand your market. Knowing the specifics of your asset, its condition, and its market value is crucial. This knowledge will help you identify potential buyers who are interested in your assets and are willing to pay a premium. Researching similar recently sold assets can give you a reasonable idea of what buyers might be willing to pay.

Choose the correct method or medium to sell. Determine how you're going to sell. Different assets might sell better through other venues. Using various platforms to reach potential buyers can increase your chances of getting a higher price. This could include online marketplaces, auctions, dealerships, galleries, or private sales.

Set the right price, and then be patient. Set the lowest price you will accept, such as a stock limit price, reserve price at an auction, etc. Selling an asset for the highest price often requires time and patience. Finding the right buyer who is willing to pay your asking price might take time. You will have to decide whether you want to create competition by setting a low price and stoking desire among competing buyers. Alternatively, you could put a hoped-for price and exercise patience; this works best if you are patient in a rising market and have time.

Make the asset presentable without wasting time or money. Cleaning and making minor repairs can often increase an asset's value. However, it's important not to spend too much on making improvements that won't significantly increase the asset's value.

Take professional-quality photos. High-quality photos can make your asset more appealing to potential buyers and will often result in a higher price.

Depending on the asset, you might benefit from getting professional help. Brokers, appraisers, or online platforms can provide valuable assistance in reaching potential buyers and negotiating the sale.

Selling Collectibles

When my mother passed, she had a house full of collectibles; however, before she passed, she asked my family to find homes for her treasures. What surprised me was the things we found after carefully reviewing what I thought was junk. For example, she had gold pens, silver utensils, a beautiful piano, and many intangible childhood memories for each of us.

So, from my experience, be careful about what you perceive as junk. If you inherit a property, be careful to find homes for treasures you see; it could greatly reward you. When you remodel, consider whether you can sell rather than discard any items such as appliances or old doors. Finally, you may want to donate salvageable items to charities and claim a tax deduction. Finding homes for old stuff may be good not only for your wallet but also for the planet.

A family in southern France discovered an old painting in their attic. Imagine their surprise when Eric Turquin, a painting expert, told them it was a seventeenth-century work by Michelangelo, valued at $135 million. The piece depicts the biblical heroine Judith slaying an Assyrian general.[37]

While clearing out her deceased sister's modest suburban home in London, a woman discovered a Chinese vase in the attic. An auction house estimated the vase's value at 1.2 million pounds. The vase sold for $83 million. The vase had been made for Emperor Qianlong at the zenith of Chinese porcelain-making.[38]

Once, I went to an antiques store and was surprised at some of the items they sold. The store displayed old doors, sculptures, cameras, barware, clocks, pottery, paintings, books, comic books, silverware, and old chairs.

If you can identify dealers or collectors who might be interested in your collection, consider selling directly to them. This option may be quick and easy because you would not need to list, market, or ship the items.

---

37. ABC News, "17th-Century Painting Found in Attic Could Be Worth $135 Million," *ABC News*, April 13, 2016, https://abcnews.go.com/Lifestyle/17th-century-painting-found-attic-worth-135-million/story?id=38363620#:~:text=French%20expert%20Eric%20Turquin%2C%20who%20retrieved%20the%20painting,euros%20%28about%20%24135%20million%29%2C%20according%20to%20the%20AP.
38. CBS News, "Chinese Vase, Found in Attic, Fetches $83M," *CBS News*, November 12, 2020, https://www.cbsnews.com/news/chinese-vase-found-in-attic-fetches-83m/.

Consider selling directly to collectors through online marketplaces. This gives you access to a large, diverse audience of buyers seeking collectibles. Some marketplaces to consider are eBay, Amazon, Etsy, and Ruby Lane.

If the collectible is rare and valuable, consider using an auctioneer. Auctioneers often sell to collectors and investors. If demand is high, auctions can yield soaring prices when bidders become competitive and excited.

Sell Overly Concentrated Positions

My father used to say, "If you can't sleep at night, you are taking too much risk." That advice may be quite different for everyone, but perhaps it is the right way to think about risk. You should think about a position in the context of what it means to you. Also, if a position has grown so large that it comprises a meaningful portion of your net worth or causes you significant stress, it may be time to diversify. Overly concentrated positions may lead to substantial gains or losses. Significant losses can have psychological effects such as depression or anxiety.

You may want to sell small portions of your concentrated position to diversify into different investments. You could use the equity in your concentrated position to acquire uncorrelated or even negatively correlated investments. Correlated investments move together in the same direction. Negatively correlated investments move in opposite directions. This could help you diversify your wealth and manage your risk. For example, if you own equity in a technology company, you could borrow against or sell a portion of your investment and purchase bonds or real estate, which would have a low correlation with your equity holding. Consider scheduled stock selling on a monthly or quarterly basis.

On the other hand, you may be able to avoid taxes by either exchanging or borrowing against an asset instead of selling it outright. Loans are generally not taxable. So if you can safely borrow against your assets and invest the appreciation in other assets, this may be a great solution. In some jurisdictions, such as the US, you may be able to exchange an asset to avoid taxes.[39]

39. The United States has various tax exemptions for exchanges, including real estate (1031 exchange) and annuity exchanges (1035 exchange). Consult a qualified tax professional for further information.

Sell Your Junk and Buy Productive Assets

You may have heard of junk bonds. A junk bond is a high-yield bond that is rated below investment grade (i.e., below BB+ by S&P and Ba1 by Moody's). Junk bonds have a higher risk of defaulting. If the bond defaults, it stops making payments, and the company goes into receivership. The company's assets are liquidated, or it will be reorganized; however, bondholders may lose money.

For our purposes in this chapter, junk is any asset, not necessarily a bond, that is not likely to return the principal you invested.

For example, a company with a current ratio below one does not have sufficient current assets to cover its current liabilities.[40] Current assets are highly liquid assets that will be collectible within one year. Current liabilities are due within one year. Suppose the company also has an obsolete product lineup and so much long-term debt that no one would lend to it. In that case, the company will likely go out of business, and it is unlikely to survive. Any investment that is unlikely to survive is junk.

Also, significantly overpaying could turn an appreciating asset into junk. During the late 1990s, internet stock prices rose based on the number of clicks their websites received. Cash flow and revenue no longer mattered because the internet was going to revolutionize everything, and internet companies were hot. If everyone wants the investment, and the assumptions seem illogical or untrue, then it could be a bubble, and the investment may be junk.

Although blockchain technology may be revolutionary, I believe Bitcoin will eventually prove to be a bubble. Yes, I may be out of touch, and I have missed out on gains. However, I would rather miss out on gains that do not make sense to me than lose a significant amount by trying to sell an investment to a greater fool than me. If it doesn't make sense, don't buy it.

If the price you are paying is so high that a return to historical averages, or

40. The current ratio shows whether a business has enough cash and other short-term assets to cover the bills it must pay over the next year. Current Ratio = Current Assets / Current Liabilities. Take everything the business owns that can turn into cash within a year, and divide it by the bills it must pay within that same year. A ratio of one or higher means the business has enough liquid assets to cover its short-term obligations.

ratios of prices to cash flows, would result in a significant loss to you, avoid the investment. Avoid junk, because it may be hard to recover from losing principal.

Avoiding junk investments will save you from making costly mistakes. You may be better off choosing a lower-risk investment that will return the principal. Avoid trendy investments you don't understand well enough to purchase early in the trend. Otherwise, you may overpay for the investment. Avoid it if you cannot determine whether an investment is likely to return your principal.

Focus on investments in companies that make products or services you buy and understand. If you would like to invest in something but do not clearly understand the investment, consider investing additional time and/or money in your education until you can determine whether you are likely to get your principal back.

When you invest in productive assets, your money is put to use, theoretically benefiting society. Examples of productive assets include businesses and investment real estate. They provide a return to you, whether or not you sell them. Ideally, you want to invest in cash flow-producing assets that continually grow over time.

When you invest in anything that is not productive, you are hoping that someone else will pay you more for that asset in the future, and the money you invest really provides no benefit to society. Remember, intrinsic value is based on cash flow, so the value of nonproductive investments is the gamble that someone will pay more for them.

Warren Buffett addressed speculative traps in his 2011 shareholder letter: "[A] ssets that will never produce anything, but that are purchased in the buyer's hope that someone else—who also knows that the assets will be forever unproductive—will pay more for them in the future. Tulips, of all things, briefly became a favorite of such buyers in the 17th century."

Speculative traps require an expanding pool of buyers who, in turn, invest because they believe the buying pool will expand still further. Owners believe that others will desire it even more avidly in the future.

On numerous occasions, Mr. Buffett has stated that gold and Bitcoin are prime examples. Nonfungible tokens are another example. In the future, other nonproductive assets will become popular for a time. Remember that this can be like playing a game of musical chairs; you lose if you are standing when the music stops. Instead of playing musical chairs, invest the bulk of your wealth into productive assets.

Buy Assets That Grow and Pay!

Even in steadily growing economies, diversifying across uncorrelated, productive assets will increase cash flow over time. Here are some examples of asset classes that could provide minimally correlated cash flows: stocks, bonds, annuities, real estate, private businesses, and retirement plans. The benefit of uncorrelated cash flows is that when one source dries up, the others are likely to remain. Within each asset type, it would be wise to diversify into fifteen or more individual investments.

Allocation to Less Correlated Assets and Cash Flow

You will want to be mindful of correlations among asset classes. Correlation measures the degree to which two investments' prices move in the same direction over time. A value of 1 (or 100 percent) indicates that the assets are perfectly correlated and are moving in the same direction and by similar magnitudes. A correlation of -1 (or -100 percent) means that the two assets move in opposite directions: When one rises, the other falls by a similar amount. For example, you buy $1,000 of a S&P 500 ETF, and that ETF doubles over the next year. You also owned $1,000 each of the following: Treasury bonds, investment-grade bonds, leveraged real estate, and gold. If the correlation holds (it is never exact), you might get gains and losses as follows: $20 gain in Treasury bonds, $420 gain in investment-grade bonds, $150 gain in leveraged real estate, and a loss of $80 in gold. That is why a mutual fund that invests in stocks, Treasuries, and corporate bonds will have a less volatile price than one that invests only in stocks, because the underlying price changes differ.

The problem with correlation is that it tends to break down when you need it the most. During times of crisis, most risky assets tend to decline in price together. For example, stocks, corporate bonds, and real estate all produced negative returns during the 1931 and 2008 bear markets. In 1931, even Treasury bonds produced negative returns. Only short-term Treasury Bills produced positive returns in both years. This is because there are periods when everyone is simultaneously scared, so nobody wants to take on risky assets during those periods.

When discussing correlation, it is essential to remember that we are only considering resale prices; we are not factoring in the amount of cash you will receive if you have no intention of selling. However, cash flow will bring you closer to financial freedom than price speculation. If you have sufficient cash flow to cover your expenses, you will be less concerned about fluctuating asset values and more worried about the reliability of future cash flow. Revenue will directly impact future cash flow; however, asset values may not. Planning for adequate cash flow will make your retirement planning more straightforward and conservative.

Whether you achieve financial freedom through cash flow sources or asset values, you will want to diversify. Either on your own or with the help of a financial advisor, create a range of acceptable allocations to your chosen asset classes, and then stick to that range.

Diversification: Enough, But Not Too Much

Broad diversification occurs when an investor who does not understand the economics of specific businesses nevertheless believes it is in his interest to be a long-term owner of American industry. That investor should own a large number of equities and space out his purchases. On the other hand, if you can "understand business economics and to [sic] find five to ten sensibly priced companies that possess important long-term competitive advantages, conventional diversification makes no sense for you."[41]

41. Warren E. Buffett, chairman, Berkshire Hathaway, Inc., "Letter to Shareholders," March 1, 1993.

Mr. Buffett implied that the average investor should invest in low-cost equity index funds. Although Mr. Buffett's advice regarding buying individual stocks is extremely aggressive, the logic seems to be that the more companies you own, the less you will know about each company. I believe that for the average long-term investor, a portfolio of low-cost index funds and private real estate is best.

Minimum Level of Diversification

You can achieve nearly optimal diversification with just fifteen to thirty individual investments, depending on the level of correlation between them. When you buy a mutual fund, the fund's responsibility is to manage risk. Therefore, beginning investors can manage their risk by investing in mutual funds.

When you buy individual stocks or ETFs, avoid overconcentrating in any single industry. If stocks are uncorrelated (for example, different industries or sectors), fewer will be needed to achieve the optimal level of diversification. If you want to reduce your risk, consider adding uncorrelated investments that you clearly understand. Suppose your objective is to become as rich as possible. In that case, you will want to keep the number of investments closer to fifteen and choose investments you clearly understand that have extraordinary risk-to-reward profiles. Overconcentration may lead to tremendous gains or losses that would be hard to recover. As risk increases or expected returns decline, you will want to exchange investments. Finally, you should diversify across investments to reduce specific risk, across asset classes to reduce systematic risk, and across liquid and illiquid investments to reduce cash-flow and liquidity risk.

Diworsification

Peter Lynch coined the word diworsification in his book, *One Up on Wall Street.* If you hold all your investments in one asset class, such as stocks, you can likely benefit from diversifying across asset classes with different risk profiles; however, diversification has become such a buzzword that most people end up engaging in diworsification instead.

Diworsification is the addition of investments that worsen the risk-to-reward ratio. Essentially, investors typically add lower-return, higher-risk, or higher-fee assets to their portfolios to diversify. For example, let's say you buy an ETF that invests in every stock in a particular industry; you would own the market leader, laggards, and possibly even companies that clearly will not survive.

My father invested only in mutual funds, and he did quite well; however, he owned many managed funds, which reduced his risk across fund families but increased his management fees and potentially reduced his returns. The problem was that each mutual fund followed a different strategy, resulting in ownership of a broad range of stocks. So why didn't he just buy index funds and save on fees? By owning fifty managed mutual funds with high management fees, he likely underperformed an index fund due to the large number of stocks, turnover costs, and other expenses.[42] Overpaying for management fees may reduce your long-term performance; however, the most important thing is that you are investing and making money. If paying a manager helps you stay invested or lets you sleep at night, then they have earned their fees.

Real Estate

Andrew Carnegie famously said, "Ninety percent of all millionaires become so through owning real estate. More money has been made in real estate than in all industrial investments combined."[43]

Unlike financial assets that are managed for you, real estate is a tangible asset you can control. Real estate provides easy access to other people's money through loans without raising money from investors, and this may be why most self-made millionaires made their first million dollars by investing in real estate. Leverage may increase returns after appreciation, cash flow, and amortization. Amortization is the loan repayment plan and a source of return because you build monthly equity. Real estate provides a hedge against inflation and typically holds

42. Turnover costs are costs related to buying and selling within a portfolio, such as commissions and taxes associated with sales.

43. "Andrew Carnegie Quotes," *Goodreads*, https://www.goodreads.com/quotes/9118668-ninety-percent-of-all-millionaires-become-so-through-owing-real.

its value. Finally, real estate offers tax benefits that can shelter your income and boost your after-tax returns.

Real estate returns are primarily driven by appreciation, inflation, and tax benefits. If a population is growing in an area, then demand for housing increases. Additionally, inflation causes rental rates and property values to rise. Meanwhile, the value of debt falls with inflation, and the payment remains the same, so overall cash flows generally increase. The federal government encourages people to become landlords through tax benefits such as debt deductions, depreciation, and tax deferrals (e.g., a 1031 exchange in the US).

Why Is Debt a Benefit of Real Estate?

Globally, debt offers several benefits to responsible, savvy investors. As we discussed before, leverage may increase your rate of return. In addition, borrowed money is not taxable; therefore, you can pull money out of your investment without selling and pay no taxes. While interest is deductible as a business expense, amortization is not. Some investors use interest-only loans for this reason, so they do not have to pay taxes on the money they pay to a lender to repay their loan. Worldwide, governments do not tax loans because they represent a debt that you must repay, not an increase in your net wealth.

Refinancing an investment property can be a smart move from a tax perspective. Refinancing is not a taxable event. First, you get to tap into your property's equity without selling it, so you avoid capital gains tax (i.e., tax on appreciation upon a sale). When you refinance, you can deduct the interest as an expense, lowering your taxable income. Additionally, depreciation gives you another way to reduce your taxable income. And let's not forget about potentially securing a lower interest rate, which means more money in your pocket each month. Each person's situation is unique, so it's always wise to chat with a tax professional or financial advisor before making big decisions. For US real estate investors, I have included general tax benefits to discuss with your tax professional in Appendix A.

Recognizing the Trend in the Real Estate Market

Cash flow pays the bills, but most money in real estate is generally made from paying down leverage and realizing equity from appreciation. Thus, well-timed purchases and sales can dramatically increase the profitability of your real estate investment. So how do you recognize the current trend and the best time to purchase or sell?

First, there is a yearly cycle in residential real estate. Many families do not want to buy or sell during the school year. In the US, winter tends to create a yearly cycle of lower prices and lower volume from late fall through early spring.

Comparing property prices sold over time can show the current trend in your market. This is important to observe because if you are trying to buy or sell, it can help you decide on the appropriate price. For example, if the market is dropping, you might be able to offer a lower price as a buyer; and if you are selling, you may want to start by asking for a lower price. In other words, a buyer who offers market price in a swiftly rising market will likely be outbid, and a seller in this market may be able to ask a higher price if they're willing to exercise patience.

On a longer-term basis, seven factors affect real estate prices and timing: inflation, interest rates, inflows or outflows (i.e., current popularity), local job growth, migration, the direction of growth in the local area, and new construction.[44] Inflation and interest rates affect overall real estate attractiveness. As a long-term investor selecting an area to invest in, you should primarily consider local job growth and the direction of that growth. Sell or exchange properties in declining areas, and buy in affordable, growing, or improving areas.

The Value of Creativity

Real estate provides an essential resource for businesses and individuals alike. As such, it is always in demand. If you can provide that resource in an attractive way, you will have customers. For example, James Lee Clayton made at least $600 million by providing quality living spaces at a lower cost.

44. Craig Hall, *Timing the Real Estate Market* (2004).

Mr. Clayton made his fortune by manufacturing, financing, and selling mobile homes. He started out selling cars in the Knoxville, Tennessee, area, but he expanded too fast and filed for bankruptcy in 1961. Five years later, he purchased a mobile home retailer and renamed it Clayton Homes. Mr. Clayton built up the retailer. Four years later, he established a factory to build mobile homes. In the next four years, he began financing the mobile homes. By 1974, Mr. Clayton was building, retailing, and financing mobile homes. By 2002, he had built a mobile home empire worth over $600 million through the power of compounding.

Term Life Insurance

Mortality risk is the possibility of dying before achieving your financial goals. You may protect against the risk of mortality by purchasing term life insurance until your assets can provide for anyone who depends on you. Mortality risk is a risk to anyone you may leave behind, so you do not need life insurance if you do not support anyone. On the other hand, if you have a risky job and a lot of dependents, it would be irresponsible not to have life insurance.

When I was in the army, I knew a colonel and a captain who had families, and unfortunately, they both passed away. Although they had insurance, their wives had little experience with finances. Both spouses should understand finances and have insurance if they have dependents. If you are concerned about those you will leave behind, set up your estate to reduce the legal burdens on your beneficiaries. During plane or helicopter turbulence, I often think about my loved ones. Take care of estate planning now. If today is your last day, you will have a certain level of peace.

Estate Planning and Your Legacy

Estate planning can be complex and is beyond the scope of this book, except to note that it may be crucial to prevent the government from claiming assets nobody knows about and save your loved ones from considerable difficulties after you pass.

Find a responsible, reputable attorney and accountant in your area, and get your estate planning done right. Please consult an attorney and have them draft estate planning documents in your area. Consult your tax accountant about various taxes, costs, and income before finalizing your estate planning documents. Appendix C provides additional information for estate planning in the US.

Lasting Legacies in Uncertain Times

History shows that even during extreme crises, such as hyperinflation or regime change, families who owned productive assets preserved their wealth. Their strategies comprised two-layer portfolios, including *insurance* and *enterprise*. The insurance layer helps you survive storms, like precious metals, life insurance, or property insurance. The enterprising portfolio creates real wealth by investing in productive assets. Together, a portfolio comprising insurance and enterprise will not just survive, but will help you support your family, friends, and your community.

An enterprising portfolio uses leverage, skill, and patient capital to build durable wealth. Productive assets worth owning include farmland, factories, equipment, water rights, timber rights, industrial land, and essential services such as energy and transportation. Ideally, these assets retain the ability to provide goods and services, including food, energy, products, and transportation. The idea is to own assets that will be needed regardless of the political regime in power. During inflationary environments, prices rise while long-term fixed-rate debt loses real value, meaning those who own productive assets with fixed-rate leverage build real wealth. Productive assets also generate tax revenue, making their owners economically useful to whatever government holds power. This is a subtle but meaningful protection against expropriation. For all these reasons, the combination of insurance and productive enterprise has proven remarkably durable across centuries and political systems.

Conservative long-term leverage can be a powerful tool in this context, but it demands discipline. Long-term fixed-rate debt benefits borrowers when currency values debase. Short-term floating-rate loans, by contrast, may worsen a crisis precisely when stability matters most. Expertise in managing these assets is not always required. Families have successfully owned productive assets by engaging experienced, trustworthy operators who brought the knowledge the owners lacked.

The following historical examples show how, when monetary and political order collapsed, those who held real productive assets flourished, while those who held paper claims were ruined:

- **Rome:** In the ancient world, Roman elites anchored their fortunes in latifundia. Latifundia were large agricultural estates that produced grain, oil, and wine. Agricultural property that feeds people is an enduring store of value, so long as the productive capacity is preserved. After the chaos that ensued from the fall of the Western Roman Empire, many late Roman landowning families in Gaul and Italy retained substantial portions of their estates and local influence. In this way, landowners and their descendants preserved their wealth and capacity to support dependents and surrounding communities.

- **Germany:** In the early 1920s, industrial groups that controlled productive capacity and export channels initially prospered and fared better in the monetary collapse than holders of paper claims. For example, Hugo Stinnes accumulated a fortune by borrowing massive sums of money to acquire real assets such as mines, factories, and shipping lines, and repaying the loans with near-worthless currency. A generation later, the productive capacity that protected these fortunes was devastated by World War II. Many wealthy families fled with what they could carry, hence the value of gold.

- **The Soviet Union:** After the Soviet collapse, a handful of well-connected entrepreneurs moved swiftly to seize the assets that mattered most in a failing state: oil, gas, minerals, forests, factories, ports, and the transport networks that moved them. Privatization turned these strategic assets into private empires almost overnight, creating the oligarch class. With weak courts and a collapsing state, these new owners relied on private security and criminal rackets to defend what they controlled. The lesson was brutal and simple: In a failing state, productive assets are the only wealth that matters.

These disparate examples distill into a handful of enduring principles. Maintain some cash or "dry powder." When using muskets, soldiers had to keep gunpowder dry to fire their muskets. Similarly, you need some liquidity to act when others cannot. Diversify geographically so that no single political or economic collapse can reach everything you own. Use fixed-rate, long-term debt conservatively, understanding that it will amplify both gains and losses. Engage experienced, trustworthy local operators to extend your reach across asset classes you cannot manage alone. Finally, build a reputation for integrity, because in times of crisis, relationships and trust become their own form of capital.

The goal is straightforward: Preserve wealth, compound real returns, and endure. Families who have accomplished this throughout history shared common disciplines: 1) They kept their insurance portable, 2) owned what society could not do without, and 3) governed their capital with prudence. That combination did not merely allow them to survive the storm. It allowed them to emerge stronger.

Check Your Knowledge

1. What does your personal balance sheet consist of?
2. What are ways to increase your assets?
3. What asset characteristics help you achieve financial freedom?

Chapter Summary/Key Takeaways

First, assess your current personal balance sheet.

Next, avoid investments that are unlikely to return your principal.

Consider whether you should sell off part or all of any concentrated positions at the best possible price.

Use other people's money if you find an extraordinary opportunity.

Diversify with three to six asset classes: the less correlated, the better. Then diversify with fifteen to thirty investments within each asset class.

Buy productive assets that provide cash flow and growth.

Once you have achieved substantial wealth or have an heir, hire a responsible, competent attorney and accountant, and set up your estate.

CHAPTER SIX:

Receive Real Risk-Adjusted Returns

Money makes money, and that money makes money.
—Benjamin Franklin on compound interest

Real Returns Rule

Think of real as net returns. The real returns rule is to maximize your net returns for any given level of risk.

Edward Thorp was a portfolio manager, author, and mathematics professor who specialized in modern probability theory. Mr. Thorp's most famous book was *Beat the Dealer: A Winning Strategy for the Game of Twenty-One*. His system tried to determine when the odds are in your favor. Bet more when the odds are in your favor and less when the odds are not. To simplify the gist of his card-counting strategy, it was all about weighing risk against reward.

Obviously, you would prefer the highest possible returns for any given level of risk, but investments carry the risk of loss. Additionally, you will likely keep less than your gross returns. You care about what you keep, not what you gross; you care about real, not nominal (i.e., total) returns. Taxes, inflation, expenses, and risk may reduce your total (i.e., nominal) returns. So your goal should be to maximize your results by considering what you keep and then considering anything that reduces the amount you keep.

The purpose of this chapter is to demonstrate ways to increase the net returns you keep without increasing risk. If your portfolio's average real returns were consistently negative due to inflation, taxes, depreciation, expenses, and/or risk, your portfolio could not grow. By mitigating the effects of factors that reduce your net returns, you may increase your real risk-adjusted returns.

Increasing Real After-Tax Returns Without Increasing Risk

In the bustling city of Prosperity Valley, two men, John and Steve, set out on their investing journeys with dreams of comfortable retirements.

John, a STAR student, had done his homework. He carefully divided his assets based on tax efficiency. Inside his tax deferred individual retirement account ("IRA"), he traded actively, taking advantage of tax-deferred growth on short-term market opportunities. He held tax-efficient long-term investments outside his IRA, including index mutual funds, individual stocks, and private real estate. John benefited from lower capital gains tax rates and untaxed appreciation.

Steve, on the other hand, was extremely cautious. He avoided risk, parking his money in bank CDs, convinced that safety meant prosperity. Steve skipped the tax advantages of an IRA, not realizing that these taxes were avoidable. Real estate seemed too complicated, so he steered clear.

Years passed. John's tax-efficient strategy allowed his investments to compound significantly without frequent tax hits. His real estate holdings appreciated, providing passive income and inflation protection. When he retired, he had a diverse portfolio. He traveled the world, enjoyed fine dining, and donated generously to causes he cared about.

Steve, meanwhile, faced a cruel reality. His bank CDs barely kept up with inflation. Outside of an IRA, the government took half of Steve's earnings. He retired to a modest lifestyle and struggled to afford necessities. Eventually, he became frustrated by rising costs. His savings shrank faster than anticipated, and the golden years he'd imagined turned into a constant battle against expenses.

Avoiding risk isn't always safe. By smartly balancing tax-efficient assets outside an IRA and tax-inefficient ones inside, you can shield your returns, grow your wealth, and ultimately enjoy financial independence.

You can reduce your taxable income with clever allocation without reducing your returns. Owning real estate provides tax-free cash flow through depreciation and loans, but real estate is illiquid. Liquid assets readily convertible to cash can be significant for meeting necessities or capturing opportunities that require money. Generally, you want tax-efficient strategies for liquid assets outside an IRA and tax-inefficient strategies inside an IRA.

Five ways to increase your returns without increasing your risk include the following:

- Reducing the effects of inflation
- Reducing or removing risk
- Employer matching
- Reducing taxes
- Reducing investment expenses

The difference between nominal and real returns is significant. Nominal returns are unadjusted returns; be careful, as these may be the advertised returns. Because there are many tax brackets, reported nominal returns will differ based on each investor's tax rate. Additionally, nominal returns do not reflect inflation. Finally, your holding period will affect both your risk and returns. Real returns matter because they compound and grow. What matters is not what you earn but what you keep. You should aim to maximize inflation-adjusted after-tax returns, not nominal returns before tax. So let's explore ways to reduce taxes, fees, and the effects of inflation.

Inflation

We all remember a time when something we liked cost less. If you live long enough, those memories can be pretty dramatic. As long as governments issue currency, they will inflate it. Benjamin Franklin said, "Nothing is certain in life but death and taxes." Inflation is a form of taxation. The inflation rate depreciates a currency's future value, so an accurate return is the return you get, excluding inflation. The real return reflects the actual return in today's dollars. Let me illustrate how inflation affects two businesses: 1) without pricing power, and 2) with the ability to pass expenses to its customers.

Imagine you decide to start an online store selling 3D printed parts. You invest $100 to buy materials and set up your website in the first year. At the end of the year, you earn $130 because you sold the parts for $230. Inflation begins to creep in, raising material costs by 10 percent annually. In the second year, you buy the same amount of materials for $110 and sell the same amount. Due to inflation, you earn $120 because you could not raise the price due to competition. Unfortunately, when you spend your earnings, you find that everything else has gone up in price too, so your profits don't go as far. This pattern continues into the third year, with inflation rising by 10 percent, and you are worse off.

Consider a business such as rental properties that can pass inflation along to the consumer. For simplicity, we will assume fixed expenses. In year one, the cost is $100; the earnings are $130 because the rent is $230. In year two, the rent increases to $253, so your profit is $153, but those profits are worth $139 of things you could have bought in year one. In year three, the rent increases to $273, so your profit is $178. However, those earnings are only worth $147 in terms of what you could obtain in year one; therefore, your real return shows that you are better off than when you started due to inflation.[45]

By incorporating inflation into the scenario, you can see how your business's value changes over time, depending on your pricing power. In the same way, money depreciates over time.

45. $1.78 divided by 1.1 (i.e., 10 percent inflation) to the power of two years = $147.

Real risk-adjusted returns consider not only the balance of risk and reward but also how inflation erodes the actual value of earnings. This means you need to assess whether the risk is appropriate and how much your earnings will buy in the future compared to today. When you estimate a risk-adjusted return, you seek to identify the highest return for a given level of risk by measuring and comparing risk to reward.

Considering risk is essential because pursuing high returns is one way investors become victims of fraudsters or suffer severe losses. As Gordon Gekko said in one of my all-time favorite movies, *Wall Street*, "Greed is good" because it facilitates capital formation and enables companies to sell their stock at high prices, reducing their cost of capital. However, investors should first be conscious of the risk they are taking. There are ways to increase the after-tax actual returns without increasing risk, and we will discuss these methods first.

Risk Management: Retain, Reduce, or Remove Risk

When I was in the army, I learned that we should manage risk rather than avoid it. When I enlisted, my stepfather, a wise World War II airborne sergeant, told me, "Don't be a hero. Discretion is the better part of valor." Avoiding danger is sometimes the most sensible thing to do. You can and should manage risk to the best of your abilities.

Valor means great courage in the face of danger. I once met an outstanding young soldier who ran across a battlefield through a barrage of gunfire to pull another soldier out of a burning Humvee. I asked him, "How did you get the courage to do what you did?" The hero replied, "I could not live with myself if I let my friend burn." I have never forgotten his wise words. He quickly made the assessment and wisely saw the long-term cost of not taking what most would consider an unacceptable risk. He managed the risk by taking the enemy by surprise and running as fast as possible; he succeeded and remained uninjured. Ultimately, the army awarded him the Bronze Star.

There are many diverse types of risk you will face over your lifetime; some are good, and others are bad. A good risk has a reward that far exceeds the potential harm. A bad risk has little reward and unmanageable risk. The primary risks we will consider are risks that may inhibit exponential growth.

You may choose to retain, reduce, or remove risk. You may choose to retain the risk, or bear it yourself. You may want to keep certain risks, such as market risk, because you are seeking returns. Reduce risk by taking steps to lessen the likelihood and impact if they occur. (For example, you might reduce the risk of premature death by eating right and exercising.) Remove or transfer risk to someone else by buying insurance or options. (For example, you might reduce the risk to your family of your premature death by purchasing adequate term life insurance.)

Risk to your earnings or income may affect your ability to obtain exponential growth if you withdraw principal to cover living expenses. Your health can impact your ability to work, so stay healthy by eating healthy food and exercising regularly. Exercise first thing in the morning so you get it done. Cook your own food so you can control the ingredients.

At work, give your best effort. For example, be on time and do not try to do other things while working. Improve your skills so you can be a star performer. Businesses fail sometimes, so have a plan B. Think of where you could work or what you could do if you lost your income. In addition, you should always have enough liquid, lower-risk investments to cover anticipated living expenses to transition to plan B.

Devastating financial losses due to property or liability risks could affect your ability to achieve exponential growth, so mitigate these risks. Property risk is the risk of loss due to damage, destruction, or theft. Liability risk is the potential for damages or harm to another. Mitigate property and liability risk by self-insuring or purchasing insurance. When you buy insurance, you are pooling your money and trusting an insurance company to handle that money responsibly, so choose an insurance company wisely. Choosing a high deductible will reduce your insurance cost but still cover you against catastrophic losses. Additionally, you may self-insure by setting aside a monthly replacement fund and investing it in a mutual fund. As your self-insurance fund builds up, you may eliminate any traditional insurance you purchased.

If you run a business, you may further protect yourself from liability risk through a corporation. Since a corporation is a separate legal entity, you may not be liable for losses beyond the amount you invested; however, this is not always the case. For example, if you commingle personal and corporate assets, or if you commit fraud, you may be personally liable despite forming a corporation. Different corporations have different tax benefits, so talk to your tax preparer and attorney before forming a corporation.

Longevity risk is the potential to live longer than your financial assets can support. You can buy insurance against longevity by purchasing an annuity, which is an insurance product that helps reduce the risk that you will live longer than anticipated and run out of money and allows you to defer taxes on the amount invested. Remember that all insurance costs money; therefore, those costs may inhibit the growth of assets. A low-cost plain vanilla annuity offers tax deferral when purchased outside a qualified plan (e.g., a regular brokerage account). Purchasing an annuity within a qualified account (e.g., an IRA) renders the tax-deferral benefit redundant and may not make sense. If you have saved sufficient assets for retirement, never using your principal may be a simpler and better option. If you purchase financial assets, vary your spending to adjust for returns above annual inflation. Withdrawing only excess returns will ensure you never run out of money.

Employer Matching

One of my coworkers once told me that he did not contribute to our employer's 401(k) plan, which matched the first 8 percent of contributions. I remember feeling frustrated as I explained that he was giving up free money. As a young man, he was potentially giving up millions of dollars. In the first year, he gave up a 100 percent return on his investment in the form of an employer match.

Since he was in his early twenties, he was also potentially giving up forty years of returns, which could have amounted to millions of dollars in returns offered but not taken.

Peter Thiel and the Magic Roth IRA[46]

In 1999, Peter Thiel was chairman and CEO of PayPal. PayPal paid its founders small salaries coupled with stock. Mr. Thiel purchased 1.7 million shares at $0.0001 per share, or $1,700, and put them into a Roth IRA. Reportedly, he never contributed to his Roth IRA again. According to multiple news sources, Mr. Thiel's Roth IRA was worth as much as $5 billion in the summer of 2021. Since Roth IRAs are tax-exempt after contributing, he should be able to withdraw the entire sum tax-free, saving him billions of dollars in taxes. Mr. Thiel's story illustrates the power of exponential growth and the tremendous tax savings of a Roth IRA. Many countries offer tax-deferred accounts similar to Roth IRAs in the US. I recommend consulting a tax accountant who is familiar with tax laws in your area and can recommend appropriate tax-free or tax-deferred accounts where you live. For US investors, I have included a summary of current retirement accounts in Appendix B.

Where Should My Investments Be Held?

Ideally, you want to use high-return, tax-inefficient strategies within tax-deferred or exempt accounts, and use tax-efficient strategies outside of those accounts. For example, covered call strategies are ideal within tax-deferred accounts because they generate many taxable transactions. Real estate, index funds, and long-term stock holdings can be great investments outside of tax-deferred accounts.

You care about your net returns. In taxable accounts, your net return includes nominal returns minus the effects of taxes, fees, and inflation. In tax-deferred accounts, only fees and inflation serve to reduce your nominal returns.

46. Alessandra Malito, "How Peter Thiel Turned $2,000 in a Roth IRA into $5,000,000,000," *MarketWatch*, June 24, 2021, https://www.marketwatch.com/story/how-peter-thiel-turned-2-000-in-a-roth-ira-into-5-000-000-000-11624551401.

While evaluating your investments, consider ways to reduce your taxes and save more money legally. First, contribute to tax-deductible savings accounts such as retirement or health savings accounts. These accounts allow you to save pretax dollars, reduce taxes, and increase compound returns compared to taxable accounts. Second, outside of tax-deferred accounts, choose tax-advantaged investments such as real estate, untaxed bonds, or annuities. Third, don't sell taxable investments. Generally, sales are taxable worldwide. However, most jurisdictions allow access to appreciation without taxes, such as through loans. Additionally, US investors may be able to exchange one investment for another under certain circumstances, so you should consult a qualified tax professional in your jurisdiction to discuss tax planning.

Tax-inefficient strategies should be executed in a tax-deferred or tax-free account. Ideally, a Roth IRA will employ a high-turnover strategy (buying and selling frequently). Traders may dramatically increase their short-term net returns by trading inside a tax-deferred or tax-free account.

Execute tax-efficient strategies inside taxable accounts. For example, a taxable account should hold annuities, nontaxable bonds, individual stocks, real estate, or index funds that have been purchased and held for the long term. The longer the holding period, the more tax-efficient the equities become. No sale means fewer taxes. Real estate is another highly tax-efficient investment. In the US, annuities are tax-deferred financial contracts with insurance companies. *Do not* buy annuities inside a tax-deferred account. When you own tax-efficient investments inside a tax-deferred account, the tax-deferral benefit is redundant, and you may be incurring substantial additional costs that will be a drag on your portfolio's performance.

Reduce Investment Expenses

While grocery shopping, you might compare prices and quality. Similarly, you should comparison shop for investment and management services. Annuities and mutual funds have prospectuses that state their fees; however, there are simpler ways to find these essential numbers than by reading these complex, dense documents. Here are four sources to easily review these critical numbers:

1. Morningstar compares investment companies on various factors, including expenses.
2. Many brokerages offer summaries of their products, including expenses and costs.
3. FINRA's website (https://tools.finra.org/fund_analyzer/) offers a mutual fund calculator to compare fees and in-depth information about mutual funds.
4. If you need more detail, prospectuses and annual reports are available through the companies, the SEC's EDGAR website (https://www.sec.gov/edgar/search-and-access), or your investment representative.

Reduce the Effects of Inflation

Inflation slowly erodes the value of money. Remember when the things you purchased were cheaper? Unfortunately, inflation is here to stay. Governments have historically inflated their currencies, from the Roman Empire to the Chinese Dynasties. Inflation benefits society by creating the impression of prosperity; however, it hurts currency savers and benefits borrowers. The value of money depreciates, reducing the value of savers' financial assets, including debt; therefore, borrowers repay lenders with less valuable money. So how can you protect yourself?

Certain assets, such as real estate and stocks, benefit from mild inflation. One way to protect yourself is to become a borrower and purchase tangible assets such as real estate. When you buy a home, you lock in the amount you will pay for shelter. This is a hedge against rising housing costs. When you buy a real estate rental with positive cash flow, your tenant pays off the mortgage. Companies can set prices when demand for their products is strong. These companies can pass inflation on to their customers through price increases. Typically, real estate, precious metals, and stocks appreciate as inflation rises, which may make them good long-term investments.

For US investors, the Federal Reserve publishes a wide variety of valuable economic data on its website, including inflation data.[47,48] We typically measure inflation by changes in the prices of a basket of goods and services, known as the consumer price index (CPI). The CPI and inflation are published on the Fed's website.[49]

Good portfolio management can seem complex, but it can be simplified by focusing on risk versus reward. To achieve the highest possible returns, you must be as flexible as water. Choose the asset class that offers the least resistance to achieving your goals. Your strategy should focus on choosing the asset classes with the best expected risk-adjusted returns.

Investment Horizon Buckets

Think of investments as different buckets of money that you'll invest with specific goals. When will you need to spend the money? An emergency or opportunity fund should be available immediately. However, the money you want to bequeath to your children may have an investment horizon that's longer than your life. Generally, invest in the following three buckets to maximize real return for the risk:

1. For one- to five-year goals, choose money market funds holding short-term government or corporate debt. These funds are for emergencies and extreme opportunities, so the funds need to be accessible immediately.

2. For funds you'll need within six to ten years, choose mutual funds holding long-term corporate bonds and government bonds, or buy them individually.

3. For goals that are ten years out or longer, choose equity mutual funds or

47. *Federal Reserve Bank of St. Louis,* https://www.stlouisfed.org/.
48. *Board of Governors of the Federal Reserve System,* https://www.federalreserve.gov/.
49. "Inflation, Consumer Prices for the United States (FPCPITOTLZGUSA)," *St. Louis Fed,* https://fred.stlouisfed.org/series/FPCPITOTLZGUSA.

exchange-traded funds, stocks, real estate, and precious metals. (This is not an all-inclusive list.)

Whatever investments you choose, you should understand them, including both risk and potential rewards.

Since you want to maximize the real return for the risk you are taking, you will invest in different assets depending on when you may need access to the principal.

If you have the luxury of keeping assets that you may never use, stocks and real estate would be my choices since these assets have historically held their values over the long term and provided cash flow.

The amount that should be in each bucket depends on your life, willingness, and ability to take risks. How much income does your portfolio need to provide each year? If you are working, then that depends on the security of your job and whether it provides for all your needs. While you are working, you will want to have enough assets in low-risk investments to cover six months to a year of expenses in case you lose your job.

When you retire, you will need a steady cash flow to cover your costs. Add your dependable sources of cash flow for the year and deduct your expenses; the result is your yearly surplus or shortfall. The more cash flow your assets provide without liquidation, the more you may invest in risky assets. Multiply your annual shortfall by ten, and invest this amount into a ladder of bonds or bond ETFs, and you should never have to draw from risky assets for necessities unless you want to. A bond ladder is a series of bonds that mature in different years. The bond ladder returns principal when needed, while not investing more than is necessary.

Risk-to-Reward Ratios

Another factor that makes the risk-to-reward ratios better for stocks and real estate over long-term investment horizons is the average compounded return or expected value. In other words, the amounts and frequency of losses diminish with time with both stocks and real estate, while average returns increase. Long-term, leveraged real estate and stocks have the highest nominal rate of return and the fewest losses. Unleveraged real estate returns have historically low volatility but low returns, so 50 percent leverage was used.[50] The nominal average return on bonds has historically been low; thus, it can depress returns, even resulting in real long-term losses. Therefore, a seemingly conservative portfolio held for the long term may be riskier than conservative equities or real estate.

The average can be quite attractive over long investment horizons. Investors without an edge should focus on selecting appropriate asset classes for their investment horizon, and on reducing fees, inflation, and taxes to boost returns. A long-term portfolio of index funds and private real estate should perform well. Short-term portfolios should consist of low-volatility assets so you can use the money as you intend.

For various time horizons, I analyzed the effects of returns and inflation on risk-to-reward ratios across asset classes from 1928 to 2022.[51] The results are contained in the graphs below. I adjusted cumulative returns for inflation, so these are the real risk-to-reward ratios. These graphs show that both stocks and leveraged real estate delivered higher long-term risk-to-reward ratios. On the other hand, fixed-income investments struggled to keep up with inflation, making them riskier for the returns provided over long investment horizons.

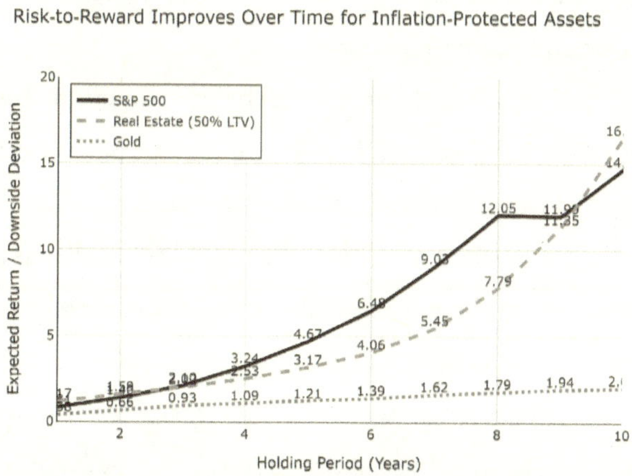

50. For the purposes of this analysis, I assumed an average real estate leverage of 50 percent, and I assumed that tenants paid all expenses, so the only factors considered were leverage and appreciation.
51. Data obtained from New York University is believed to be reliable. To review the source data, you may visit the following website: https://pages.stern.nyu.edu/~adamodar/New_Home_Page/home.htm.

Risk-to-Reward Is Low Long Term for Fixed-Income Assets

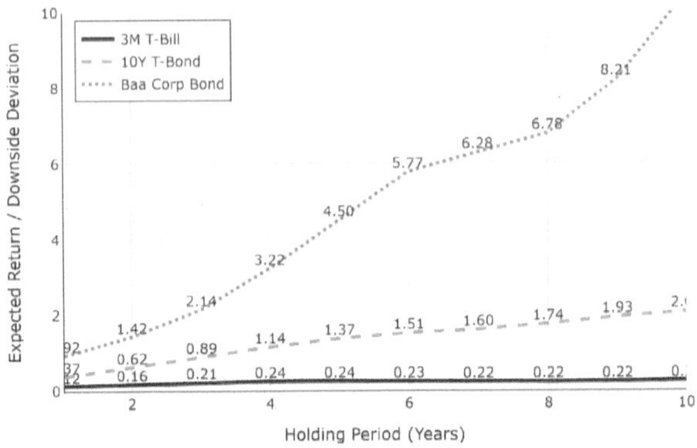

Inflation ate away at the principle for bonds, and the returns were not significant enough. Additionally, for longer investment horizons, the number of instances in which an investor would have lost money by investing in a diversified portfolio of stocks or real estate decreased to nearly zero. In general, assets hurt by inflation deteriorated over time, whereas assets helped by inflation improved.

Inflation is less of a concern in the short term than volatility; therefore, short-term goals may be better served by bonds. For investment horizons of less than five years, in the worst historical instances of inflation outpacing bond returns, investors lost as much as 25 percent of their purchasing power for short-term bonds and 30 percent for long-term bonds.

Investors who purchased stocks or gold just before a significant historical bear market lost more than 50 percent of their real purchasing power during the next five years. If forced to raise cash quickly, real estate faces a similar problem due to its illiquid nature. For short-term goals, this could be disastrous as the funds would need to be used at the worst possible time to sell, thereby permanently locking in the investor's losses.

So far, we have discussed risk-to-reward in terms of the risk of losing your initial investment versus inflation-adjusted returns. Let us explore some other methods for managing your risk and/or reward.

Minimum Criteria or Buy Rules

Always set minimum buy criteria. Your minimum buy criteria are checklists. They are your shopping lists. Have you ever gone to the grocery store, hungry and without a shopping list? When I do that, I always end up with stuff I do not need. The same is true for investing.

In fund-type investments, you are delegating the purchase of individual investments to someone else, so dollar cost averaging is an excellent choice, but you still need to decide which fund to buy. You should look for the lowest-cost, low-turnover liquid funds that fit your objectives for index and exchange-traded funds. For managed funds, you want the most skilled manager. Ask how the manager is compensated to determine if their interests are aligned with yours. For money market funds, you want low-risk tax-exempt funds outside a tax-deferred account and a higher-yield taxable funds inside.

For individual stocks, I look for quality, undervalued businesses. By quality companies, I mean growing firms with some form of competitive advantage. The company should be the low-cost provider of a commodity-type product (i.e., one that people purchase primarily based on price). Alternatively, the business should have robust brand recognition so customers will continue to buy their products. By undervalued, I mean companies with a low price-to-cash-flow or earnings ratio that are growing quickly or recovering from financial hardships. Furthermore, I will only buy shares that I expect to double in value within the next three years to ensure safety. Sometimes, prices take a while to reflect their actual value, so I generally allow the stock three years to adjust. Since I am not an insider, I want to see that insiders believe in the company and are net stock buyers in the last three months with positive cash flow.[52] I prefer small-cap stocks because their limited number of shares can cause dramatic price swings.

For real estate, you want rental properties that break even with 50 to 80 percent leverage. You should compensate yourself for management. Generally, if you can purchase a property with positive net cash flow at current rents and

52. This is publicly available information through the SEC's EDGAR database.

50 to 80 percent leverage, you have found a sound investment. Estimate the rent for each unit using Zillow or another website, then subtract a vacancy allowance. I usually use 10 percent for estimated vacancies, but that will depend on your area. Then subtract your remaining mortgage, management fees, taxes, insurance, utilities, services, maintenance fees, and replacement costs.[53] The result is your net cash flow. If cash flow is positive, you will likely have an excellent investment. Your profit is determined by how well you made your purchases.

Sell Rules

When should you sell? This can feel like a puzzling question. If you've made a truly excellent purchase, the answer may be rarely. Even so, someone could make an irrationally high offer for a fantastic investment; this would be an exception to the rule of never selling an excellent investment. Most of the time, you may find that you made a mediocre investment, so it may help to have preestablished selling rules.

For selling stocks, you must decide how well you know the company and industry you are investing in. You may not want to sell extraordinary companies with excellent economics during your lifetime. If you hold the position until you pass, you may bequeath the stock tax-free in the United States. In that case, nobody will ever pay taxes on the gains if you are not subject to the estate tax. For every stock position that you are uncertain about or do not know well, you may want to establish a trailing stop loss. Some people like to keep these trailing stop losses in mind, fearing that brokers will execute trades if they are on their books.

For fund investments, you may want to sell for several reasons. Sell fund investments when the manager changes and you do not have confidence in the new manager. If you buy index or exchange-traded funds, you must decide how much you want to allocate to that specific asset class. Sell when the allocation to that asset class exceeds or falls below a given percentage (for example, 10 percent).

53. Maintenance and replacement costs are different in that maintenance is the routine average costs of repairs that typically happen during the year, while replacement costs may happen during your holding period but occur infrequently and include large items like roofs (i.e., capital expenditures).

Generally, market average returns can be handsome over the long term, but there are periods of highly inflated prices that can result in extreme short-term losses and low long-term returns. If you invest in assets in a bubble, you will likely achieve low long-term returns or incur losses.

Avoiding Bubbles

Bubbles are periods of soaring prices that have little basis in cash flow or growth. Speculators drive prices by betting that prices will continue to rise. When everyone else seems to be making a fortune in the popular investment of the day, it can be tempting to follow the crowd. A bubble can start as a solid idea with cash flow and potential growth; however, if there are rapid price increases, widespread speculation, and heightened investor enthusiasm, beware: you may be in a bubble. Instead, focus on buying assets with significant cash flow and growth potential. If you are lucky enough to purchase an investment before a bubble, you should sell enough to take out your principal and a reasonable profit, then risk the amount you are willing to lose.

Although digital currency and blockchain may in fact be the way of the future, I believe Bitcoin may be an extraordinary bubble. If you find this topic interesting, there is an excellent book called *Extraordinary Popular Delusions and the Madness of Crowds* that covers the mass psychology of bubbles.

The Importance of Edge

You do not need to beat the market to become wealthy, but if you're going to try to beat the market returns, you'll need an edge. Traders and arbitrageurs seek to exploit short-term price discrepancies.[54] They increase the frequency of compounding and, in turn, the total number of periods. Profitable trading can increase returns; however, short-term price movements can be challenging to predict. It might seem like a clever idea to trade more in an attempt to increase your compounding frequency, but it may be counterproductive. So there must

54. An arbitrageur connects buyers to sellers who are present at the same time but in different places and prices, such that the arbitrageur can profit by acting as an intermediary.

be a balance between trading frequency and risk-to-reward ratio. If you are going to trade more frequently, make sure you have a good reason. If you trade, you should have an edge.

Richard Dennis was a phenomenally successful commodities trader who turned $1,600 into over $200 million. Mr. Dennis is famous for conceiving the turtle trading experiment. In 1983, he taught students with no trading experience to become expert traders. The novice investors (turtles) earned $175 million in five years by following a trend-following strategy taught to them by Mr. Dennis. The turtle trading experiment demonstrated that anyone could become a successful investor through a disciplined, systematic approach.

Curtis Faith was one of Mr. Dennis's trading students. He wrote, "An edge in trading is an exploitable statistical advantage based on market behavior that is likely to recur in the future."[55] Mr. Faith wrote about turtle trading rules in his book, *The Way of the Turtle*. He was one of the most successful turtle traders, making Mr. Dennis over $31 million while he was a turtle. Turtles were not day traders; they were trend followers. They traded frequently to keep their losses small, but when they identified a trend, they held the position if it persisted.

Holding on to winning positions rather than taking quick profits is a common theme among many of the world's most famous traders and investors, such as John Paulson. Mr. Paulson famously made $15 billion for his firm, Paulson & Co., by betting against subprime mortgage-backed securities (MBS) during the housing crisis. He held these positions for years, which must have taken considerable courage and conviction.

Whether you are investing for the long term or trying to beat the market, it is all about the risk-to-reward ratio. If you obtain real positive returns, then your assets will continue to grow and compound over time.

---

55. Curtis Faith, *The Way of the Turtle* (2007).

Check Your Knowledge

1. How can you increase your real risk-adjusted returns without increasing your risk?
2. If you need your money soon, which investments are more appropriate?
3. For exceptionally long investment horizons, which investments are more appropriate?

Chapter Summary/Key Takeaways

You should aim for the highest possible real risk-adjusted return, which reflects the actual return in today's dollars after accounting for risk. Here are several ways to increase returns without increasing risk:

- Take advantage of employer matching
- Use tax-free or tax-deferred accounts
- Hedge against inflation
- Reduce fees
- Increase risk-to-reward ratios
- Use appropriate investment horizons
- Remember that you do not need to beat the market to become wealthy
- Keep in mind that beating the markets is possible, but you will need an edge

PART TWO:
APPLYING STAR

CHAPTER SEVEN:

Two Roads to Riches: Funds and Real Estate

Failing to plan is planning to fail.
—Benjamin Franklin

The plan that is right for you will depend on your unique circumstances, risk appetite, assets, and objectives; the following examples are for illustrative purposes only.

Bob and Susan's Traditional Plan

Bob and Susan want to know the earliest date they can retire while minimizing risk during retirement. After setting aside six months to a year of emergency reserves, Bob and Susan, both aged twenty-five, start saving as much as they can in their 401(k) accounts. Their living expenses are $90,000 a year, and they expect that to remain the same in retirement, adjusted for inflation. We will assume that projected inflation and the risk-free rate are both 3.5 percent. Bob and Susan invest 100 percent in equity mutual funds, and their average annual return is 9 percent.

Even without employer matching, Bob and Susan could retire at forty-eight to sixty-three years old, but if their portfolio underperforms their expected return, they may run out of money. They could retire at age forty-eight or older if 100 percent of their investments remain invested in equities. At age sixty-three or older, they could invest all their money in risk-free assets and never run out of money. As this couple ages, their expenses increase with inflation, but their life expectancy declines. The more conservative the couple wants to be in retirement, the more money they will need. Bob and Susan's plan could succeed because they have a long-term horizon, tax-deferred compounding, and higher returns than inflation.

The chart below illustrates Bob and Susan's retirement plan with portfolios designed to last until age 120. The black, upward-curved line represents their projected retirement account balance while they are working. The lower line represents the minimum net present value (NPV), so they will not run out of money if they invest aggressively in all equities. The middle area represents portfolios with returns that are lower than equities but higher than the risk-free rate. The top line is the portfolio after retirement if invested in risk-free assets. The chart illustrates the trade-off between risk and the total assets needed to achieve financial freedom; portfolios with lower risk require more assets.

Bob and Susan's plan could work, but they could improve it. Also, it would not work for many people. First, it requires twenty-three years, but they could save more. Second, they started young, but most people do not. Third, not everyone has access to a 401(k). Fourth, their plan is vulnerable to high inflation. Finally, Bob and Susan could run out of money if their portfolio underperforms projections.

Bob and Susan's Real Estate Rentals Plan

What if Bob and Susan invest the same amount in rental properties with positive cash flow after building up six months to a year of emergency reserves? The chart below plots their living expenses compared to their cash flow from real estate. Bob and Susan agree to purchase only properties with a maximum price of ten times the rent and positive cash flow. Assuming rents continue to rise at or above the rate of inflation, Bob and Susan should have a secure retirement. In this projection, Bob and Susan acquire eight rental properties over fourteen years, generating at least $5,000 in free cash flow per year. By the time they are thirty-nine years old, Bob and Susan's cash flow grows to $144,000 annually, exceeding their inflation-adjusted living expenses. After they reach their financial goal, their cash flow and lifestyle may continue to improve with inflation. This plan would require Bob and Susan to work hard, execute well, and stay focused, as with any plan.

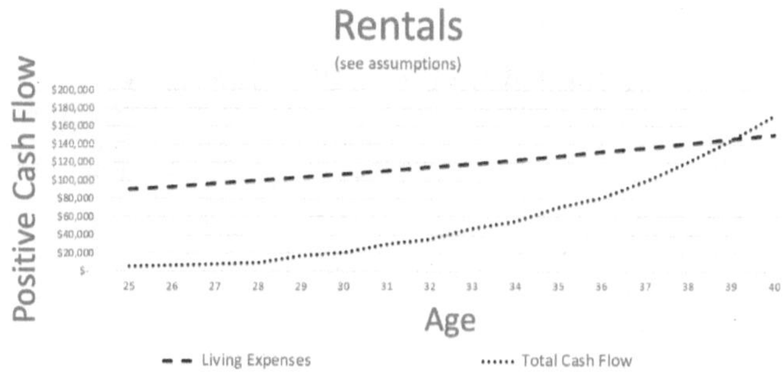

Let's discuss some assumptions and disadvantages that are not obvious in the real estate example. First, real estate can be very illiquid. Therefore, selling real estate is not a good option if you need cash quickly. Second, this scenario assumes an initial loan-to-value ratio of 80 percent and the ability to raise rents in line with inflation; however, properties may not generate positive cash flow with that much debt when interest rates are high. Third, local laws can make rental properties unattractive. For example, many California cities have imposed strict rent control and restricted rent increases, yet they have done nothing to prevent landlords' costs from rising. Fourth, real estate and stocks can become overvalued or undervalued, making it challenging to purchase them at reasonable prices at times. Fifth, depending on the area, a tenfold gross rent multiplier (GRM) may be unrealistically low or applicable only to hard-to-sell properties.[56] Combining real estate rentals and stocks is the best approach for long-term investment horizons.

If you can obtain decent rentals in your area with GRMs of ten or less, it may be best to keep properties for a long time. In these areas, people often buy single-family homes or small apartment buildings because they are easier to manage and offer strong appreciation potential.

If your area has only properties with GRMs above ten, you might need to be more creative or more patient. You might need to buy properties that need some repairs or upgrades so you can raise the rent and increase the property's value. In these markets, buying apartment buildings is often better because you can spread out your costs over more units. You could try living in one part of the property and renting out the rest. You could also focus on luxury, flipping, short-term rentals, or mixed-use properties.

Accelerating the Rental Business

If Bob and Susan have trouble saving for down payments, they could buy their first house with FHA financing and only 3.5 percent down if they have credit scores of at least 580 (as of 2025). Furthermore, living in additional properties for the time required by their lender (usually one year) would reduce the initial down payment to 10 percent; however, the increased debt would reduce their cash flow.

Buying a four-unit building to start may accelerate Bob and Susan's plan by reducing their living expenses, enabling them to save more toward their next rental property, and/or contribute significantly to a traditional 401(k). Additionally, by utilizing two- to four-unit buildings, Bob and Susan may reduce the

56. As of January 31, 2026, the average arithmetic mean of one hundred sampled metropolitan statistical areas (MSAs) was 9.4; however, it is very challenging to find properties with such low GRM numbers in areas like Southern California. For more information, see https://apartmentpropertyvaluation.com/gross-rent-multiplier/city.

impact of vacancies, increase cash flow, and increase the total number of units owned; eight four-unit buildings would total thirty-two units upon retirement.

David M. Greene authored an excellent book, *Buy, Rehab, Rent, Refinance, Repeat,* which discusses how to accelerate your real estate acquisitions. The book recommends buying fixers, but instead of flipping them, increasing the rents, renting them out, pulling out your initial investment by refinancing, and then repeating the process. Essentially, you free up the capital you invested in to do the next deal. When interest rates drop or rents increase, refinancing will give you another opportunity to improve your cash flow and/or tap your equity. When you pull out your initial investment but maintain a positive cash flow, your rate of return may increase dramatically because you have nothing invested in the property.

After you have completed a few successful deals, people may be interested in investing alongside you. Friends and family members may provide capital to continue your real estate journey. Today, there are even crowdfunding portals that may enable you to raise funds for deals that you could not do by yourself. If you reach that level, you have become a professional investor, which is beyond the scope of this book.

Raising Risk-Adjusted Performance?

The Sortino ratio refines risk-adjusted performance by penalizing only downside volatility (i.e., returns below a chosen minimum acceptable return, or MAR), rather than all volatility.[57] That focus makes it a superior metric when the investor cares chiefly about protecting their long-term objectives. Adding private real estate to a diversified long-term portfolio may significantly improve the portfolio's Sortino ratio.

Although the long-term, nominal rate of return of equities is historically higher than that of unleveraged real estate appreciation alone, private leveraged

57. Frank A. Sortino and Lee N. Price, "Performance Measurement in Portfolio Management: The Sortino Ratio," *CFA Institute*, accessed November 8, 2025, https://rpc.cfainstitute.org/sites/default/files/-/media/documents/code/gips/the-sortino-ratio.pdf.

real estate adds the following complementary qualities to a diversified portfolio of equity mutual funds and precious metals over long-term horizons:[58,59]

1. **Income and amortization:** Private properties receive returns from net cash flows and debt amortization. These returns are uncorrelated with market prices, thereby improving portfolio Sortino ratios.

2. **Diversification and inflation hedge benefits:** Real estate valuations are usually uncorrelated with the stock market and gold. Additionally, real estate values benefit from inflation.

3. **Liquidity premiums:** Private real estate may offer an illiquidity premium with smart purchases that may reward long-term investment horizons.

4. **Active management:** Investors may add value through leasing, repairing, remodeling, and financing private real estate.

5. **Tax benefits:** Appreciation and income may be shielded from income taxes.

From 1970 through 2025, a diversified portfolio could have achieved a higher Sortino ratio than any single asset class. Combining equities, precious metals, and leveraged real estate potentially increased returns per unit of downside risk. Best practices include conservative leverage and sufficient liquid assets to prevent distressed sales.

Investors in private real estate should be conscious of the following risks, which are not all-inclusive:

- Leverage amplifies both upside and downside.
- Appraisal-based returns may smooth returns.

58. Morningstar Research, "The Role of Real Estate Investments in a Portfolio," *Morningstar*, January 11, 2023, https://www.morningstar.com/funds/role-real-estate-investments-portfolio.
59. "The Benefits of a Diversified Private Real Assets Portfolio," *Brookfield/Oaktree*, July 2023, https://www.brookfieldoaktree.com/sites/default/files/2023-07/The-Benefits-of-a-Diversified-Private-Real-Assets-Portfolio.PDF.

- Illiquidity requires deliberate management to avoid forced sales, which could result in severe losses.

Using the straightforward plans outlined in this chapter may result in financial freedom; however, you can do better. As long as your plan adheres to the principles of STAR, it may work. Take a moment to imagine how applying STAR to your life could create the freedom you desire.

Check Your Knowledge

1. Using a 401(k) and mutual funds, why does Bob and Susan's plan work?
2. Using real estate, why does Bob and Susan's plan work?
3. Why is it best to combine approaches?
4. How can Bob and Susan accelerate their plan?

Chapter Summary/Key Takeaways

Bob and Susan explore two approaches to achieving financial freedom: one using mutual funds and 401(k)s, and the other using rentals and hands-on property management. The keys to their success depend on their execution and future market returns.

If Bob and Susan choose the retirement account mutual fund approach, they need to focus on the following elements:

- Building enough of a reserve (probably about six months of living expenses) to be able to find a job
- Staying employed and focusing on contributing as much as possible to tax-deferred accounts
- Choosing funds, such as equity mutual funds, that will return significantly more than inflation over the long term

- Extending their time horizon until they have sufficient assets to retire comfortably (or dividend cash flow from stable, growing companies sufficient to cover their expenses)

If Bob and Susan choose to focus on real estate, they will build a business.

- Build a reserve of at least six months of reserves per unit. This may be conservative, but it will also protect against unexpected repairs.
- *Only* buy when a property can deliver a positive cash flow net of all expenses, capital expenditure reserves, and financing.
- Do not buy in areas that have overly restrictive rent control laws. Even in California, some places are less stringent and some property types are at least partially exempt.
- Extend your time horizon until you have sufficient cash flow to cover your desired lifestyle.
- Three methods to accelerate your real estate journey include:
    1. Starting with a multiunit building
    2. Referring to *Buy, Rehab, Rent, Refinance, Repeat*
    3. Raising money and becoming a professional investor

Investing long-term in equities and private leveraged real estate may lead to high Sortino ratios due to cash flows, amortization, low correlation, and illiquidity premiums. Long-term investors should consider holding both equities and private, leveraged real estate to increase returns for a given level of downside risk.

CHAPTER EIGHT:

Fiduciaries and Fraud Defense

Trust but verify.
—Russian proverb, recited by Ronald Reagan

That is fantastic advice when you're considering whether to hire a broker or advisor. Being skeptical can be beneficial. Nobody cares more about your wealth than you do. Some so-called investment professionals are not as talented as others. Some are just looking out for themselves. Finally, if your advisor or broker does not increase your returns by more than their fees, they will reduce your returns; furthermore, the additional costs may substantially reduce your long-term performance. A good broker or advisor can make the difference between good returns and disaster. To reinforce that concept, here is a short story.

Fred Fiduciary[60]

The conference room was quiet except for the sound of Fred Fiduciary flipping through pages of his report. Mr. Fiduciary's team had spent months investigating one of the most sought-after investments on Wall Street, a hedge fund that had delivered high, steady returns for decades. Everyone wanted to buy the fund: pension funds, endowments, and the wealthy. Buying was a privilege, and Mr. Fiduciary felt extremely uncomfortable about his presentation.

"Something's not right here," Mr. Fiduciary said, looking at the portfolio

60. This story is fictional, and any similarity to real life events is coincidental.

managers and investors gathered around the conference table. He had founded RiskShield Diligent Advisors Incorporated (RiskShield) with like-minded colleagues specifically to conduct rigorous due diligence.

Mr. Fiduciary continued, "The auditor is one person, auditing a multibillion-dollar operation."

An investor protested. "The returns are fantastic and steady, year after year above average returns."

"That's part of the problem," Mr. Fiduciary replied. "The manager claims to move billions in various trades at once. However, there are no public footprints for the trades. Who's the counterparty? No regulatory filings are showing this activity."

Mr. Fiduciary continued reading through his team's findings. "The manager executed trades, custodied assets, and administered everything himself, with no independent oversight or risk controls. Family members held key positions. The comptroller was offshore. When we requested standard due diligence information, the fund refused."

The report set out various scenarios ranging from the operation being entirely legitimate to outright fraud.

"I can't recommend this investment," he stated.

So RiskShield's clients did not invest.

Over the next eighteen months, they watched other institutional investors pour money into the fund, and they continued to deliver steady, outstanding returns. People whispered enviously about those who had invested. Some of RiskShield's clients questioned the firm's conservative stance; some even moved their assets to other firms. Mr. Fiduciary believed that where there was smoke, there may be fire, so he kept his files updated and stood by his analysis, never investing in the hedge fund.

On December 11, 2008, the financial markets were in chaos. The government was bailing out major banks, and fear prevailed. The global economy teetered on the edge of catastrophe, and then the news broke that Bernie Madoff had been arrested for running a Ponzi scheme involving billions of dollars.[61]

Mr. Fiduciary froze in disbelief when he realized that he had been right all along, but he'd never imagined the magnitude of the fraud. Bernie Madoff, the former NASDAQ chairman and legendary investor, had confessed. It had all been a lie. For decades, Mr. Madoff had fabricated statements and confirmations. RiskShield's reputation soared when the warning became public. In subsequent interviews, Mr. Fiduciary stressed the value of asking uncomfortable questions even when everyone else wants you to stop.

The Gap Between Detection and Justice

According to the SEC inspector general's report, the agency received multiple credible warnings about Mr. Madoff's operation but did not act decisively. These warnings highlighted red flags that suggested serious risks, even if they did not independently prove fraud. Over the course of sixteen years, the SEC received at least six detailed and credible warnings about Mr. Madoff's fraud, including detailed allegations from Harry Markopolos, but failed to act decisively.[62]

Following the Madoff scandal, the SEC instituted several significant reforms to improve its ability to detect and prevent fraud. The agency overhauled its Division of Enforcement by creating specialized units, reducing management layers, and hiring industry experts to focus on complex and emerging market areas. It also revamped its approach to handling tips and complaints by implementing a new centralized electronic system and leveraging data analytics for better risk assessment, thereby prioritizing examinations of high-risk firms. Furthermore, the SEC enhanced investor safeguards by implementing new rules requiring independent custodians or surprise examinations for investment advisors and by strengthening oversight of how broker-dealers manage customers' assets. Examination practices changed with a greater emphasis on fraud detection.

61. "Bernie Madoff Case," *FBI*, https://www.fbi.gov/history/famous-cases/bernie-madoff.

62. US Securities and Exchange Commission Office of Investigations, "Investigation of Failure of the SEC to Uncover Bernard Madoff's Ponzi Scheme—Public Version," https://www.sec.gov/news/studies/2009/oig-509.pdf.

Additionally, the passage of the Dodd-Frank Act created a formal whistleblower program to encourage the reporting of securities violations.[63]

Fraud is just a fancy word for intentionally lying about finances. Think of fraud as a fire. If you saw smoke coming out of a building, would you rush in to prove there is a fire? No; you would call the fire department and stay the heck out of there unless there was an exceptionally good reason to go in. Fraudsters will attempt to get you to ignore your instincts and invest for some very compelling reasons, usually irresistibly high returns and/or negligible risk.

If you suspect fraud, you may want to call regulators or law enforcement rather than the fire department. There are bright, hardworking regulators and law enforcement officials who will do their best to find, prove, and stop fraud; but, at times, it can be difficult to detect and/or prove. Because it can be challenging to detect, tips from people with actual knowledge of fraud can be extremely helpful in protecting others from harm. Even after detection, it may take time to build a case because schemes can be complex. Regulators and law enforcement need to go in, find it, prove it, and put out the fire.

You only need to detect the smoke; you do not need to put out the fire (i.e., you don't need to prove the fraud). You only need to suspect fraud and choose not to invest. For this reason, investors should be aware of what to look for. Although fraud is constantly evolving, lies have common red flags, and if you trust your instincts, you can detect fraud!

Avoiding Fraud

An ounce of prevention is worth a pound of cure.
—Benjamin Franklin

It would be a shame to achieve financial independence only to lose it due to fraud, so let's discuss some ways to protect yourself. If you take the following precautions, you will avoid most fraud:

63. US Securities and Exchange Commission, "The Securities and Exchange Commission Post-Madoff Reforms," https://www.sec.gov/spotlight/secpostmadoffreforms.htm.

- Understand your investments.
- Be skeptical.
- Use strong, independent custodians or escrows.
- Perform a thorough background check or due diligence.
- Hire a fiduciary.
- Diversify your investments.
- If you see something, say something.

Understand Your Investments and Needs

Before hiring professionals, you should know what services you need, what they can provide, and how much they will cost you. Financial planners can help you assess your situation and develop plans to meet your goals. Full-service real estate brokers, stockbrokers, and investment advisors can recommend suitable investments for your goals. Robo-advisors are generally asset allocation services; you won't pay much, but shouldn't expect much in return. However, as artificial intelligence progresses, that may change. There may be limitations on what professionals can recommend based on their licenses. You should know what you are paying for and how much you are paying. In general, more advice means more fees. However, more fees do not guarantee better returns and will make it more difficult for the manager to beat their investment benchmark.

Thoroughly understand the strategies being employed on your behalf, and regularly review your assets and any transactions being conducted. If you receive statements, you should review and understand what is happening. Understand your statements and choose a strong, independent custodian. Is the activity you see in your statements consistent with what your representative tells you? Incomprehensible explanations or inconsistencies are huge red flags.

Be Skeptical

If it sounds too good to be true, be cautious. Skepticism encourages investors to critically evaluate investment opportunities, questioning the underlying assumptions and ensuring that they are based on sound analysis rather than hype. By maintaining a healthy level of skepticism, investors can identify red flags that may indicate fraudulent activities, such as overly optimistic projections, a lack of transparency, or dubious credentials. Taking a skeptical approach ensures that investors base their decisions on facts and evidence, leading to more informed and rational investment choices. By questioning excitement and trends, skeptical investors may avoid market bubbles and speculative mania which often lead to significant losses. If you've been skeptical, kicked the tires, and still believe the investment is extraordinary, the odds are much higher that you've truly found a great one.

Fraudsters often attempt to manipulate investors and regulators by making them feel foolish, using aggressive tactics, or being overly friendly. The best fraudsters find ways to gain your trust, so "trust but verify." Over many years of interviewing, I've discovered that the best approach is to be polite and professional, and friendly but not overly so. Generally, I try to get people to relax and talk. I do not immediately confront people with apparent lies; instead, I ask for further clarification. For example, "Perhaps I didn't understand?" Sometimes, explanations and documents will alleviate my concerns. Other times, the stories get more elaborate and the records show inconsistencies. Fraud detection is about getting to the truth.

A Strong Independent Custodian or Escrow

A custodian is an entity, such as a bank or a clearing broker-dealer, who holds your funds and investments. It is the entity to which you write the check when you invest. Ideally, you should hold your assets at a solid, independent custodian. Always write a check directly to the custodian. Diversifying among custodians could also protect you against losses caused by the custodian's financial problems.

Ensure that you trust your custodian, as custodian fraud (such as Bernie Madoff's) can result in the loss of your entire investment. Remember, Bernie Madoff ran a large, highly respected firm, but he had custody of the funds. Review your advisor's compensation. Ensure that the custodian you choose has either Securities Investor Protection Corporation (SIPC) or Federal Deposit Insurance Corporation (FDIC) insurance. If your broker or advisor is not a custodian, you should never write a check to them. This information can be found in your advisor's investment brochure (Form ADV Part 2A) and Form CRS.

For US brokerages, the SIPC provides insurance to protect customers if their brokerage firm fails. The coverage limit is $500,000 per account on securities and $250,000 on cash. SIPC insurance guarantees that you will receive your securities back, but it does not insure you against declines in value while the settlement process plays out. If your account exceeds $500,000, verify whether the custodian has private insurance. You may also want to consider opening other accounts with different custodians and/or multiple accounts.

Working with custodians with strong balance sheets and adequate insurance will reduce your total investment risk. Custodians generally make their balance sheets publicly available on the SEC's EDGAR database. Private insurance will help to protect your assets, and in the US, you may have SIPC or FDIC protection. A custodian with a strong balance sheet will likely never need SIPC or FDIC insurance. In addition to reviewing the balance sheet, check whether the auditor is a reputable firm.

Check whether the auditor registered with the Public Company Accounting Oversight Board, or PCAOB (https://pcaobus.org). Auditors who audit broker-dealers registered with the SEC must register with the PCAOB. Auditors who only review investment advisors generally do not need to register with PCAOB. You can verify PCAOB membership on their auditor search (https://pcaobus.org/resources/auditorsearch). This is a public database of engagement partners and audit firms participating in audits of US public companies.

A good independent custodian will protect you against losses due to the mishandling of your funds. Never write a check directly or indirectly to your financial advisor. Only write checks to well-capitalized, audited custodians. An independent custodian will also protect you by issuing monthly statements so you know what is happening in your account. An advisor who uses an independent custodian cannot affect the statements, because custodians mail statements directly to you. Demand and review statements from audited (preferably independent) custodians you have faith in.

In real estate, similar advice may apply. Check your escrow company on the Better Business Bureau. Verify the escrow company's license in your state. Verify phone numbers, and never change wiring instructions or other sensitive information in response to an email. Document every step of the transaction with secure communications. Be suspicious of unsolicited requests to change wiring details.

If you have decided to employ a broker or advisor, check their background before investing with them.

Background Research on Brokers or Advisors

Suppose you want help from an advisor or broker. There are honest professionals, if you know where to look. If you can focus on your life and feel less stress, then perhaps the fees are well worth the money spent. In that case, you need to determine whether they are experts and professionals by conducting thorough background research. Verify any claimed licenses or credentials. Some of the worst fraudsters lie about licenses and credentials, hoping you won't check. Review their track record. Verify safeguards, such as independent custodians or pay that aligns with your goals. Finally, look for a pattern of complaints with regulators. Many times, multiple investors complain before regulators have time to put a stop to a scheme.

You should verify that the person is appropriately licensed through resources such as FINRA's BrokerCheck[64] for stockbrokers, the SEC's Investment Adviser Public Disclosure (IAPD)[65] for advisors, your state's respective real estate

64. "BrokerCheck," *FINRA*, https://brokercheck.finra.org.

65. "Investment Adviser Public Disclosure," *US Securities and Exchange Commission*, https://adviserinfo.sec.gov.

department for real estate, and your state's department of insurance for insurance products. Avoid anyone who is unlicensed or has a history of complaints.

Ask about their credentials. For example, do they have a CFA, CPA, MBA, or PhD in finance? In my opinion, these credentials are the most respectable and demonstrate that the person has put considerable work into understanding finances. You may be able to verify their credentials on the internet. Look at their track record. Are they adding value based on their performance, or would you be better off in a no-load index fund?

Ask about their fees, then consider available services. Check competitors to see what comparable services cost. Then review their performance compared to the cost of the services offered. Will your representative's pay affect the advice they provide? Most firms will disclose these conflicts of interest. Consider any conflicts when deciding whether their advice is better for you or them.

Again, make sure your representative employs a strong, independent custodian or escrow company. Only choose broker-dealers with SIPC insurance and/or sufficient other insurance to cover the amount you will invest with them. A strong balance sheet audited by a reputable firm can provide some additional comfort.

Only hire a representative with a lack of complaints or regulatory discipline. Many investors who have difficulties with investment representatives complain to regulators. Researching representatives before you invest could save you money, obtain better results, and help keep dishonest or unlicensed people out of the financial industry. Avoid people with a history of many complaints or arbitrations. Fraudsters may be very charming and able to explain away others' complaints; however, a well-established pattern of customer complaints is a huge red flag signaling that others have had problems with your prospective broker in the past.

SEC-registered advisory firms must prepare disclosure documents for their firms called Form ADV (Parts I and II). These forms contain information about business practices and problems with regulators or clients. It also discloses the advisor's service fees and strategies.

The advisory firm must also prepare a report about your specific representative's background and disciplinary history (Form ADV Part 2B; which is different from the above forms, which cover the whole advisory firm). Form ADV Part 2B provides essential information about your prospective advisor, including qualifications, disciplinary history, other businesses, and additional compensation. Qualifications include details of their education and professional experience. Verify their credentials, as many fraudsters exaggerate or falsify their qualifications. This may be easy to detect. Form ADV should include disciplinary events that were material for the past ten years. Other business activities include compensation received from sources other than clients. Avoid institutions that pay their representatives in a way that does not benefit you. Do not hire anyone who lies about their qualifications, has many complaints, or has other businesses that cause you to question their loyalty to you.

Before hiring a new stockbroker or investment advisor, you should be able to find the information mentioned above by visiting one or more of the following resources: the investment firm's website, the SEC website, FINRA's website, and the SIPC website. For brokers and advisors, go to the investment firm's website, then download and read their customer relationship summary (Form CRS); this will give you a description of the services provided. If you are hiring an advisor, you may also obtain Form ADV Part 2B directly from the firm. Additionally, investment advisor documents can be obtained on the SEC's website (https://adviserinfo.sec.gov/). The SEC provides public balance sheets through its EDGAR database (https://www.sec.gov/search-filings). For stockbrokers, FINRA offers registration and disciplinary history for any brokerage firm and representative on their website, BrokerCheck (https://brokercheck.finra.org/). Additionally, you can verify SIPC membership on the SIPC website (https://www.sipc.org/list-of-members/).

Before hiring a new Realtor, check their membership and verify their license in your state. Realtors must follow a strict code of ethics, so check to make sure you are using a Realtor by going to the National Association of Realtors (NAR) website (https://directories.apps.realtor/?type=member). Additionally, visit your state real estate regulator's website to verify the real estate agent's license. If the person you are talking to is not a real estate agent, they are likely a wholesaler or investor. Both wholesalers and investors are principals; they are not fiduciaries, which means they are looking out for themselves and not you.

What Is a Fiduciary?

Fiduciaries are agents who are legally and ethically bound to act in your best interest, placing your needs above their own. This duty includes the following:

- **Loyalty:** Avoiding conflicts of interest and acting solely for your benefit.[66]
- **Disclosure:** Revealing all material facts that could affect your decisions.[67]
- **Confidentiality:** Protecting your private financial information.[68]
- **Obedience:** Following your lawful instructions.[69]
- **Care and competence:** Exercising professional diligence and skill.[70]
- **Accounting:** Responsibly managing and documenting your assets.[71]

In the US, these obligations are enforceable under law, including the Investment Advisors Act of 1940[72] and 29 US Code §1104.[73]

66. Legal Information Institute, "Fiduciary Duty," *Cornell Law School*, https://www.law.cornell.edu/wex/fiduciary_duty.
67. SEC, "Commission Interpretation Regarding Standard of Conduct for Investment Advisers," https://www.sec.gov/files/rules/interp/2019/ia-5248.pdf.
68. Ethics Unwrapped, "Fiduciary Duty," *University of Texas*, https://ethicsunwrapped.utexas.edu/glossary/fiduciary-duty.
69. Justia, "CACI No. 4100. Fiduciary Duty Explained," https://www.justia.com/trials-litigation/docs/caci/4100/4100/.
70. Harvard Law School, "Fiduciary Duties," https://hls.harvard.edu/bibliography/fiduciary-duties/.
71. National Association of REALTORS, "Fiduciary Duties," https://www.nar.realtor/sites/default/files/handouts-and-brochures/2014/nar-fiduciary-duty-032213.pdf.
72. Investopedia, "Investment Advisers Act of 1940," https://www.investopedia.com/terms/i/investadvact.asp.
73. US Code, "29 US Code § 1104 - Fiduciary Duties," https://www.law.cornell.edu/uscode/text/29/1104.

Why Fiduciary Duty Matters

I once reviewed a prospectus in which the investment manager explicitly stated that they were not a fiduciary. That was enough for me to walk away. Why? Because fiduciary duty is the gold standard of professional responsibility in finance and real estate. If someone doesn't owe you that duty, they may not be considering your interests.

Whether you are selling a home or investing, your decisions may involve professionals whose incentives may not align with yours. Without fiduciary protection, you may be negotiating against seasoned operators with legal teams and opposing profit-driven motives. Here are two examples:

A cash buyer offers $400,000 for your home. A fiduciary Realtor runs a market analysis and finds comparable homes selling for $550,000. Even after a 6 percent commission (approximately $33,000), you get over $500,000, or more than $100,000 above the initial offer. If you may lose your home unless you act quickly, the cash offer may be better; otherwise, it is likely not in your best interest. The Realtor may also protect your privacy and motivations.

A broker pitches a proprietary product with 12 percent returns. A fiduciary advisor reviews it and finds excessive fees, unsuitable risk, or red flags. Instead, they recommend diversified, low-cost investments aligned with your goals.[74]

While you are investing, fiduciaries may help you avoid fees that you are not aware of. In real estate, there may be assignment clauses, inspection contingencies, hidden fees, and extended closings that favor buyers.[75] Investments may contain yearly fees, front-end loads, surrender charges, and revenue-sharing arrangements that erode your returns.[76.] Fiduciaries may help you spot these traps and explain the fine print.

Sometimes, fiduciaries can unlock superior options. Real estate agents market

74. Smart Asset, "Ways Financial Advisors Breach Fiduciary Duty," https://smartasset.com/advisor-resources/breach-of-fiduciary-duty-examples.
75. Legal Clarity, "Do Real Estate Agents Have a Fiduciary Duty?" https://legalclarity.org/do-real-estate-agents-have-a-fiduciary-duty/.
76. Accounting Insights, "What Is a Fiduciary Breach?" https://accountinginsights.org/what-is-a-fiduciary-breach-key-examples-and-financial-impacts/.

your property widely, creating competition and driving up prices.[77] For example, your real estate broker should list your house on the Multiple Listing Service (MLS), which provides data to all the websites buyers use to search. Investment advisors may have access to institutional-grade investments and index funds that commission-based brokers do not promote.

For complex situations, they can tell you when to bring in attorneys or accountants. When you are feeling vulnerable, hiring a fiduciary can be particularly important to protect you from legal or financial pitfalls.[78]

Not everyone needs a fiduciary. If you're experienced, disciplined, and have time to manage your own deals or portfolio, you might not need help. Under these circumstances, discount brokers make sense. But sometimes, even a pro can benefit from a second set of eyes to catch blind spots.[79]

Hiring a fiduciary is like having a financial bodyguard. They're legally bound to protect your interests, level the playing field, and help you make smarter decisions. Whether you're selling property or investing assets, having fiduciary representation isn't just helpful; it's a smart move.

See Something, Say Something

If you witness fraud and you genuinely believe a violation has occurred, report it. Regulators' resources are finite, so credible complaints are valuable. Frivolous or speculative reports undermine the system that is designed to protect investors and maintain fair markets. Suppose you have legitimate concerns and credible information. In that case, regulators want to hear from you. Whether you're a victim seeking justice, a concerned citizen providing a lead, or an insider with detailed knowledge seeking recognition and protection for coming forward, by reporting credible issues, you may be helping regulators protect others.

---

77. Rate Simple, "Fiduciary Responsibilities in Real Estate," https://ratesimple.com/blog/in-a-real-estate-transaction-the-term-fiduciary-typically-refers-to-a-guide-to-legal-responsibilities/.
78. Syracuse University College of Law, "Issue Brief on Fiduciary Responsibilities," https://law.syracuse.edu/wp-content/uploads/IssueBriefWorkingGroup5Fiduciaryfinal.pdf.
79. Legal Clarity, "Breach of Fiduciary Duty: Common Examples," https://legalclarity.org/breach-of-fiduciary-duty-common-examples/.

Check Your Knowledge

1. What steps can you take to avoid fraud?
2. Explain the value of a strong, independent custodian or escrow company.
3. How can you investigate the background of your potential broker or advisor?
4. What is a fiduciary?

Chapter Summary/Key Takeaways

The following are steps you should take when hiring an investment professional:

- Understand your investments.
- Know what services you need.
- Be skeptical.
- Use a strong, independent custodian or escrow. Review the investments or the custodian's audit, if available.
- Conduct a background check.
    - Verify any claimed licenses and credentials.
    - Check for complaints or prior regulatory problems.
    - Understand compensation and strategies.
- Hire a fiduciary.
- If you detect fraud, do the right thing and tell regulators or law enforcement so that others may also avoid harm.

CHAPTER NINE:

You've Got This!

As higher beings, we have a choice of what we consume. Just as we choose the quality of what we eat and drink, we can also select the quality of the thoughts we consume. The quality of our thoughts directly influences not only who we are but who we become.

To become an extraordinary investor, you need the right mindset, which you will develop through practice. Throughout my lifetime, I have had many opportunities, some of which I have taken and others which I have missed. There were four personal characteristics I exercised when I was financially successful and lacked when I failed. Those four characteristics were discipline, a commitment to being informed, courage, and engagement (DICE). Discipline will help you be humble and patient, and will enable you to act when appropriate. Being curious, skeptical, and thinking independently will help you become informed and make better decisions. You will need courage to ask the right questions and to risk your capital. Finally, you will need to be engaged in saving and investing.

In the casino game of craps, the shooter has the dice. In your life, you are the shooter; you decide what opportunities to take or avoid. Your decisions and actions will determine your success or failure. So strive to be disciplined, informed, courageous, and engaged. You've got the DICE, and you're in control. Make it happen!

Disciplined

The key to investing is to be able to sit on your hands and do nothing.
—Warren Buffett

When you have found a great investment, it takes discipline to hold on to it during corrections. This is especially true with stocks. Stocks sell quickly, and you always know the quoted price. I find discipline tremendously easier to exercise with real estate. The illiquid nature of real estate means you face significant transaction costs when selling, which discourages frequent changes. By holding during corrections, you avoid taxes and capture the tremendous compounding that is possible with long-term investments, as demonstrated by Warren Buffett's career.

Having the formula for wealth or financial freedom is not enough. Saving money rather than spending it takes discipline. Discipline helps you resist temptations that could take you off course. Even when you reach financial freedom, discipline will help you live within your means.

It is natural to want what you do not already have. We all seem to want more. However, there will be many times when you will have to choose between buying something now that you cannot afford and waiting to contribute more, allowing you to comfortably purchase what you want.

My younger self wanted a Corvette. When I finally had enough saved, I went to the dealership and almost bought one. I thought, "I have the money, and girls will love it." At the time, it was all the money I had. Thankfully, a salesperson did not approach me. This was in 2003, at the bottom of the bear market. Instead, I invested the money in the stock market. Within two years, I had a couple of hundred thousand dollars, whereas I would have had no money if I had purchased the Corvette.

Living within your means takes discipline, whether you are just starting or have already achieved financial freedom. You will always need discipline to achieve and maintain financial independence. You want to be in control of your money, not the other way around, so cultivate discipline.

Tips for disciplined wealth building include the following:

- Only buy luxuries that you can afford to pay for in cash.
- Figure out how much you can reasonably save monthly, then deduct that much and invest it every month.
- Create a checklist for investing, and stick to it.
- If an investment does not fit your criteria, pass.

Informed

An investment in knowledge pays the best interest.
—Benjamin Franklin

John Paulson's story is a fascinating tale of foresight, research, and bold decision-making. During the mid-2000s, the US housing market was booming, and MBS were widely considered safe investments. However, Mr. Paulson, the founder of Paulson & Co. (an SEC-registered advisor and brokerage), saw warning signs that others had missed. He and his staff conducted meticulous research into the housing market. They realized that significant numbers of adjustable-rate subprime mortgages had been issued to borrowers who were unlikely to repay them. Investment banks packaged subprime mortgages into MBS. Mr. Paulson used credit default swaps to insure enormous amounts of MBS; therefore, when the housing market crashed, his hedge fund made an estimated fifteen billion dollars.

Mr. Paulson and his staff conducted extensive research and analysis to build the confidence to make such large bets. His team received specialized data and developed expertise in an obscure investment area. There is no doubt that they were also courageous.

Being an informed investor means understanding the risks and rewards of an investment. So here are several ways to make informed investment choices:

- Know the investment well enough that you could explain it to your spouse or best friend. If you don't, skip it.
- Read news articles and reports from people who disagree with you. If you feel the same or even stronger after reading opposing points of view, you may have a great idea.
- Prospectuses and offering memoranda usually have a risk section that details many risks you might never think about, many of which will never occur. Reading this information can be eye-opening.
- Many annual reports contain a letter on management discussion and analysis. This may give you a glimpse into management's plans for the future.

Courageous

Be fearful when others are greedy and greedy only when others are fearful.
—Warren Buffett[80]

In the early 1990s, the United Kingdom participated in the European Exchange Rate Mechanism (ERM), which aimed to stabilize exchange rates by tying currencies to the German mark. George Soros believed that the British pound was overvalued and that the UK would eventually have to devalue its currency.

Mr. Soros attributed his success to his theory of reflexivity, which he wrote about in his book, *The Alchemy of Finance*. The theory of reflexivity suggests that market participants' perceptions influence stock values. Those values, in turn, affect a firm's ability to raise capital and the cost of that capital (i.e., higher stock prices mean the cost of capital is lower, improving its ability to compete). This feedback loop drives market prices until they become unsustainable. After this

80. Forbes Profile, "Profile Warren Buffett" *Forbes*, October 4, 2025, https://www.forbes.com/profile/warren-buffett.

trend becomes untenable, it may persist for a while; however, when something forces prices to move in the opposite direction, the reversal can be pretty dramatic.

Mr. Soros shorted the British pound because it was overvalued, which in turn affected the market and ultimately led to its devaluation. He demonstrated considerable courage and conviction in his ideas when he shorted the British pound.

On September 16, 1992, the UK government attempted to defend the pound by raising interest rates and buying pounds on the foreign exchange market. The UK government had considerable resources available to support the pound sterling. However, these efforts failed, and the UK devalued the pound. According to *Forbes*, Mr. Soros and his Quantum Fund shorted $7 billion sterling and bought $6 billion mark with less than $2 billion in equity.[81] His bet paid off, earning him an estimated $1.5 billion in September 1992 and the unofficial title as "the man who broke the Bank of England."

You may need to be courageous to become extraordinarily wealthy like Mr. Soros; however, becoming financially independent requires considerably less courage. If you understand the concepts in this book and your investments, you may find that it doesn't take much courage at all. Taking too many risks may result in losing a sizable portion of your wealth and having to start over from scratch.

Several times, I found investments that I felt could make me extraordinarily wealthy. In some instances, I was right and invested some but regretted not investing more. In other cases, I did not invest at all because the fear of loss held me back. In some cases, I made mistakes and lost the money I had invested. It is best to bet on something with which you are comfortable, rather than not taking the risk at all. Although it is a slower approach, consistently making smaller bets will help you achieve financial independence without risking having to start over. You will still need courage, but not the kind required to make huge bets like Mr. Soros and Mr. Paulson.

81. Steve Schaefer, "Forbes Flashback: How George Soros Broke the British Pound and Why Hedge Funds Probably Can't Crack the Euro," January 21, 2016.

Engaged

The path to success is to take massive, determined action.
—Tony Robbins

Sara Blakely's story is an incredibly inspiring example of how "massive, determined action" can lead to incredible success.[82] In 2000, Ms. Blakely started selling fax machines door-to-door. Between 2000 and 2012, she turned a five-thousand-dollar idea into a billion-dollar empire through relentless action and creativity. One day, she was frustrated with her pantyhose and how they looked with open-toe shoes and a white skirt. She started by cutting the feet off her pantyhose, writing her own patent, and persuading a small hosiery mill to take a chance on her prototype. With no outside investors, she pitched her brand, Spanx, directly to Neiman Marcus, even changing clothes mid-meeting to prove the product's effect. Soon after, Oprah named Spanx one of her "Favorite Things," catapulting the brand into the spotlight. Ms. Blakely hustled at the grassroots level—personally moving products to better store displays, driving around with a "SPANX" license plate, and sending samples to celebrities and stylists. Over the next decade, she expanded Spanx into shapewear, leggings, and apparel, essentially creating a new retail category while keeping the brand fun and approachable.

Ms. Blakely's example demonstrates the benefits of control and "massive, determined action." By refusing outside capital, she retained full ownership and scaled through word of mouth, guerrilla marketing, and direct-to-consumer channels. By 2012, Spanx was generating hundreds of millions in revenue, and *Forbes* recognized Ms. Blakely as the world's youngest self-made female billionaire, a testament to her persistence, resourcefulness, and refusal to give up control. At the time of writing, in 2025, Spanx is an internationally recognized brand with over two hundred products.

82. Matt Stefon, "Sara Blakely," *Encyclopedia Britannica*, last modified 2023, https://www.britannica.com/money/Sara-Blakely.

Being engaged fuels motivation and commitment, increasing the likelihood of achieving your goal. Actively engaging in the process increases the likelihood of persevering through challenges and reaching your target.

Being engaged doesn't have to be hard, but you do need to act. Dreaming without taking action will get you nowhere. All the knowledge in the world will not do you any good if you fail to act. Focus on one day at a time, and the future will take care of itself.

According to Joel Arthur Barker, "Vision without action is merely a dream. Action without vision just passes the time. Vision with action can change the world."

Here are a few techniques that I use to stay motivated. I have a vision board as my computer background, and I created a short video that I watch daily to show me what I want my future life to look like. On days when you are struggling to find motivation, take an easy day, do a little, and start. Sometimes, the motivation comes after you start. Finally, promise yourself a reward for achieving your daily goals.

Check Your Knowledge

1. As you transition into becoming an extraordinary investor, what characteristics will you develop?

2. List a tip for staying disciplined.

3. What is one way you plan to stay informed about your investments?

4. Do you need to be super courageous to become financially independent?

5. How do you plan to stay engaged?

Chapter Summary/Key Takeaways

To become an extraordinary investor, take every opportunity to embody the following characteristics:

- Disciplined enough to live within your means
- Informed enough to have confidence
- Courageous enough to act
- Engaged enough to get results

As I wave goodbye, your journey must continue, and I wish you the best that life has to offer. If you feel this book would help a friend, then buy a copy for them or recommend it.

Since you liked the book enough to complete it, please take a moment to leave a five-star review so others can learn about it; unfortunately, many people negatively interpret four stars or lower, so please leave a five-star review. If you detect any errors in the book, you may contact me, and I will consider revising future editions.

CONCLUSION

God, give us grace to accept with serenity the things that cannot be changed, courage to change the things that should be changed, and the wisdom to distinguish the one from the other.
—Reinhold Niebuhr

An old man wished on the jinni's bottle to see the location of his death because he thought, "I will never go there." As much as we might like to, none of us can ever know how much time we have. Enjoy the journey, because achieving your goals and dreams will take time.

When your time comes, will you look back on your life and think it was a good life, or will you wish you had done things differently? Things may not always work out how you want them to, but if you try your best, you will not have to wonder, "What if?" Be true to yourself, and let the details work themselves out. You need to have balance because, in the end, none of us takes anything with us.

My father was a very bright program analyst who contributed to the Hubble space telescope. Still, after raising six kids on a single income and approaching retirement, he was afraid he wouldn't have enough. For ten years, he saved and learned about investments. Through leading a frugal lifestyle and investing in mutual funds, he built a sizable portfolio. My father retired early with barely enough, and he was concerned about money throughout his retirement. Although he passed away at age ninety-one, he never really enjoyed his retirement because he was always worried about money. Although he was brilliant and had much to contribute, he did not engage much with the world during retirement.

Later in life, my father confided in me that he struggled with pessimism. When he passed, I could not help but think about how sad it was that he had not enjoyed his life, money, or grandchildren more.

By contrast, my older brother was a creative, optimistic, reasonable chemical engineer. He was an accomplished medical device inventor (with more than one hundred inventions to his name) and a real estate investor. My brother was an exceptional runner and, as a young man, nearly qualified for the Olympics; he was my best man, my sounding board, my triathlon buddy, and one of my dearest friends. Even being an exceptional athlete, my brother died at age sixty-five of a massive heart attack due to an undetected issue. For a while, his death shocked and discouraged me, and his passing reminded me that we never really know how much time we have. His passing was one of the reasons I decided to retire early and finally draft this book. Because none of us is invincible, we should visit the doctor regularly for checkups. My brother enjoyed life and balanced work and time for his family and friends.

Because you do not know how much time you have, be present and live with purpose. Ultimately, how you live your life may be more important than the length of that life or the amount of money you leave for others to use. I loved my brother and parents dearly, and as much as I miss them, I believe the advice they would give is to make the most of your life.

Whatever time you have on earth, enjoy the journey and care for your body, mind, and spirit. Exercise regularly. Eat well. Visit the doctor occasionally. Learn continuously. Explore your spirituality. Set aside time for friends and family. Budget for and do things that you enjoy. Find work that is fulfilling or interesting. Make the world a better place in some way. Stay engaged by doing something that is meaningful to you for as long as you can. Please do your best to have it all, whatever that means to you.

We have discussed everything you need to achieve financial freedom and become truly wealthy; what remains is execution. Now it is up to you. You will need to apply the concepts you have learned. It may take discipline, persistence, and patience, but you can do it. Consider everything you have learned so far, and find the most direct route.

We are just stewards of the wealth we obtain, and none of us will take anything with us when we die, so live a life to be proud of, and enjoy the journey!

You can control yourself in the present moment, learn from the past, and plan for the future. Learn, earn, save, and invest. Focus on the elements of STAR that are most important to your journey. If you can envision a better future, it is within reach. Do not obsess or become attached to how it will occur.

Whatever life throws at you, remain flexible, like water. "Water's configuration avoids heights and races downward . . . Water configures its flow in accord with the terrain . . . water has no constant shape."[83] Opportunities are constantly evolving. What worked today may not work tomorrow. Learn to seize today's opportunities, because they may be gone tomorrow. Continue learning and applying innovative ideas. You may need to do things that are sometimes uncomfortable because they are new. Fight large waves, and they will overpower you; but learn to surf, and you can ride those waves.

Creating this book felt like following my destiny. Someday, you may realize that this book played a pivotal role in your journey. Always remember that money is only a means to an end. Live your dreams, and help others to live theirs. The more you make, the more you may stake. The more you give, the more you get.

May you discover serenity, strength, and wisdom to shape a better tomorrow. May your success expand without ever dimming your integrity. As your influence grows, may your spirit stay steady, your ego stay quiet, and your compass stay true. May you always be guided by virtue, humble, and honorable, even in chaos. With all my heart, I wish you the absolute best.

The future brightens with every step you take because your STAR is rising. Rise, and the universe will make way for you.

---

83. Sun-Tzu, *The Art of War*, trans. Ralph D. Sawyer (1994).

AFTERWORD:

Stability in an Age of Acceleration

Humanity is entering a period unlike any we have faced before. Artificial intelligence has the potential to become the most powerful tool ever created, capable of extraordinary alignment and/or disruption. In moments like this, stability is not a luxury; it is a necessity. Throughout history, societies have endured when they found ways to reduce fear, strengthen trust, and give people the confidence to build rather than to fight.

Governments exist to safeguard the long-term well-being of their citizens and to create the conditions for peace, order, and shared prosperity. One promising way to reinforce that mission is through sovereign wealth funds designed not as political instruments but as long-term, self-renewing foundations that grow with the economy and support future generations. Even nations without surplus natural resources can explore mechanisms that function like a national dynasty trust, investing in people rather than programs, and providing a stable minimum standard of living that reduces the fear and scarcity that drive conflict. Seen through this lens, such a framework is not a radical departure from our past but an evolution of tools we already use to create a more resilient and peaceful future.

Today's support systems can be complex, and many individuals face difficult trade-offs when trying to improve their financial footing, including the so-called welfare trap.[84] A universal baseline could simplify that support and give people the freedom to pursue work, education, or entrepreneurship without fear of losing essential support. This is not about replacing work; *it is about expanding the freedom to pursue it.* A baseline of stability empowers people to rise rather than retreat. This matters because human motivation doesn't disappear when basic needs are met; it expands.

We are wired to seek purpose, mastery, contribution, and connection. A guaranteed minimum income may reduce financial stress, but it will not diminish the human drive to build, create, and improve. History shows that when people have security, they often take more initiative, not less. If anything, it frees more people to pursue work that aligns with their strengths and aspirations, work that feels meaningful rather than merely necessary.

For centuries, economic thinking was shaped by fears of scarcity. Thomas Malthus's ideas reflected the limits of his time, but the world has changed.[85] Advances in technology, agriculture, medicine, and family planning have expanded what is possible. With global birth rates stabilizing and productivity rising, humanity now has an unprecedented opportunity to raise living standards and reduce suffering worldwide. We are no longer bound by the constraints that once defined our future. This shift in possibility also invites a change of responsibility.

"Blessed are the meek, for they shall inherit the earth"[86] might be interpreted as a call to stewardship. Perhaps it is a reminder that lasting prosperity comes from caring for the world that sustains us. The Earth is resilient yet vulnerable, and our future depends on working with our planet rather than depleting it. With today's knowledge and tools, we can choose a path that restores ecosystems, strengthens communities, and supports a thriving planet for generations to come. Inheriting the Earth means being gentle with it.

---

84. According to Necati Celik in "A Different Look at the Welfare Trap, Institutional Causes and Remedies," "a welfare recipient's reluctance and/or inability to break his/her dependence on public assistance" exists because "welfare support perpetuates the dependency of the recipient on public assistance rather than raising them to a level that they don't need assistance anymore." *American Economic Association*, https://www.aeaweb.org.
85. Prateek Agarwal, "Malthusian Theory of Population Explained," *Intelligent Economist*, April 7, 2025, https://www.intelligenteconomist.com/malthusian-theory.
86. Matthew 5:5 (The Maxwell Leadership Bible).

A sovereign wealth fund could also invest in a diversified portfolio of domestic assets, helping reduce businesses' cost of capital and strengthening national competitiveness. Such a fund would need to be built gradually and align with long-term economic capacity. To avoid concerns about government overreach, such a fund should be built responsibly; hold minority, noncontrolling positions; and operate with strict transparency and safeguards. The goal is not to direct markets but to stabilize them. To preserve the innovation and dynamism of a market-driven system while ensuring that long-term national prosperity is shared more broadly. Any such approach would require careful study and thoughtful design to minimize unintended consequences and maximize public benefit. Some countries already use sovereign wealth funds to stabilize their economies and support their people.

ACKNOWLEDGMENTS

First, I would like to sincerely thank my editors, whose expertise and guidance have been invaluable. Your dedication and hard work have helped shape this book into what it is today.

Second, thank you to my close friends and family who took the time to read and comment on my book. Your insights helped me to refine my writing, and I sincerely appreciate your efforts.

To my former SEC friends and colleagues, you taught me what it means to be professional, thorough, and skeptical. Being a part of the SEC and protecting investors was a great honor.

To those with whom I served in the military, thank you for your camaraderie, strength, and honor. So many of you taught me lessons that helped me more than you could know.

To the authors cited in the Further Reading section, each of you dramatically influenced my thoughts and development as an investor, and I am tremendously grateful to you.

APPENDIX A:

Real Estate Tax Benefits in the US

In the US, depreciation is a tax deduction for wear and tear on a building. Although depreciation represents an actual cost to the owner, it is not a cash expense. Additionally, regular maintenance extends the building's life and reduces the actual cost of wear and tear. Therefore, depreciation offers real estate investors a tax shelter for cash flow.

So a savvy real estate investor can potentially become wealthy and never pay taxes by using debt, depreciation, and deals. If you sell your home for a profit, the IRS allows you to exclude some of the profit from your taxes. You must have lived in that house for at least two out of the last five years before the sale. This exemption could save you hundreds of thousands of dollars in taxes, so it's a sweet deal if you're selling your home!

For real estate investors, a 1031 exchange allows them to defer taxes. You don't have to pay taxes if you sell your property and buy another one using all the proceeds (while following specific rules). But here's the catch: Your personal home does not qualify. Only business or investment properties qualify. Also, you generally can't access the proceeds from the sale, so you'll want to use a qualified intermediary (i.e., a special escrow company). Plus, you need to identify the property you want to buy before you sell your current property. And here's the final kick: You must complete the exchange (selling your old property and purchasing the new one) within six months. Sure, 1031 exchanges can be tricky, but they're a great option to avoid paying taxes while continuing your journey as a real estate investor.

Finally, at the end of their life, a wealthy real estate investor can bequeath their fortune to their heirs, creating multigenerational wealth. The US even allows a step-up to the current market value for heirs, potentially avoiding taxes again. As you can see, the US provides many tax benefits for real estate investors.

APPENDIX B:

2025 US Tax-Free or Tax-Deferred Accounts

A tax-deferred account shields capital gains while funds are inside the account. Tax-exempt accounts are never taxed, either prior to deposit or after withdrawal. Taxpayers can save for retirement, education, or health care and maximize the benefits of compound interest. Over the long term, tax-deferred accounts can substantially increase returns. Here are a few tax-deferred accounts available in the United States.

Tax Deferred Retirement Accounts	
Account Name	**Uses**
Health savings account	An HSA is a tax-exempt method to save for and spend on health care. This is one of the best (and most overlooked) methods of saving.
Traditional individual retirement account (IRA)	An IRA reduces the current tax bill. Taxes are deferred until withdrawal and are then taxed as ordinary income.
Roth individual retirement account (Roth IRA)	A Roth IRA is taxed before contribution. Taxes are deferred and are tax-free upon withdrawal.
529 plan	A 529 plan offers tax-deferred savings that are specifically for education.

401(k) plan	A 401(k) plan offers company-sponsored tax-deferred savings.
Thrift savings plan	A thrift savings plan is a government employee tax-deferred savings plan.
403(b) plan	A 403(b) plan is a retirement plan for university, civil government, and not-for-profit employees.
Simplified employee pension individual retirement account (SEP IRA)	A SEP IRA is a retirement savings plan designed for self-employed individuals.
Annuity	An annuity is a tax-deferred account that may supplement or replace a traditional pension. These accounts incur additional insurance-related expenses, which can be substantial.

For retirement, I think of traditional tax-deferred accounts as insurance against going broke before you die. Most of the accounts listed above are tax-deferred. If you are in a high tax bracket, most tax-deferred accounts allow for an immediate deduction from your taxes. Additionally, gains are not taxed while they are compounding. However, withdrawals from tax-deferred accounts are taxed as ordinary income.

On the other hand, Roth IRAs are wealth-building tools. A Roth account provides no immediate tax deduction; your contributions are taxed before they go in. Therefore, they offer no immediate relief if you are in a high tax bracket. However, since contribution limits are the same as traditional IRAs, you can effectively contribute more to the Roth each year. Additionally, withdrawals are not taxed. Therefore, Roth accounts that compound for many years can generate massive untaxed wealth, as Peter Thiel's story illustrated.

APPENDIX C:

Basic Tips for Estate Planning

If you live in the US and have already accumulated a sizable nest egg, you may want to set up a trust to avoid probate, dispose of assets in a manner of your choosing, and potentially provide for your legacy. Estate planning is a complex legal topic. This is just a basic overview.

A revocable living trust is like a will on steroids. While you are alive, the trust is revocable and can be amended as you see fit. When you pass, it becomes an entity with its own tax identification number, can no longer be amended, and thus becomes irrevocable. Currently, all states allow revocable living trusts, which can save your family considerable costs and heartache as they try to figure out who gets what. Before hiring an attorney, if you want a comprehensive reference guide, I recommend *The Complete Book of Wills, Estates, and Trusts.*[87]

After you accumulate the kind of wealth that prompts you to think about your legacy, a perpetual or dynasty trust may be appropriate for you. Dynasty trusts are somewhat controversial because their social impact is unclear; therefore, many states have rules against perpetual entities. (For example, where I live in California, perpetual entities are prohibited, so I have a revocable living trust.) However, several states—such as Alaska, Delaware, Nevada, and South Dakota—allow perpetual trusts.[88] Ray D. Madoff authored an excellent book titled *Immortality and the Law*, which discusses dynasty trusts in depth and whether they should be allowed.[89]

87. Alexander A. Bove, Esq., and Langa Melissa, Esq., *The Complete Book of Wills, Estates, and Trusts* (2021).
88. True Tamplin, "State Trust Situs Selection," *Finance Strategists*, May 23, 2023, https://www.financestrategists.com/estate-planning-lawyer/trusts/state-trust-situs-selection/.
89. Ray D. Madoff, *Immortality and the Law: The Rising Power of the American Dead* (2010).

From a financial perspective, let us discuss how a dynasty trust might be set up to provide for future generations. The real historical geometric average annual equity return over 142 years was 6.3 percent.[90] Providing for two additional children every 25 years, the portfolio needs to double every 20 to 30 years, requiring excess real returns of 2.2 to 3.6 percent. At an average of 25 years, there needs to be about 3 percent excess returns. While earning a real rate of return of 6.3 percent by investing in equities, you could reasonably distribute an average of 3 percent, and the portfolio may double in real terms every 25 years. If the maximum annual distribution is set below the average annual real returns, the trust and yearly distributions may grow indefinitely.

90. Online Data Robert Shiller," http://www.econ.yale.edu/~shiller/data.htm.

GLOSSARY

1031 exchange: A 1031 exchange is a tax-deferral strategy used in real estate within the United States. It allows investors to defer paying capital gains taxes when they sell a property and reinvest the proceeds into a similar, like-kind property. It refers to Section 1031 of the US Internal Revenue Code. The code requires that investors identify a new investment property within 45 days and exchange the investment property within 180 days, while never possessing any of the sale proceeds.

Adjusted gross income (AGI): The property's total rental income after accounting for vacancy allowances.

Amortization: The process of paying off a debt over time through regular payments. Each payment covers both interest and a portion of the principal amount. Over time, the portion of each payment that goes toward the principal increases, while the portion that goes toward interest decreases.

Annuity: An annuity is a structured series of equal payments made at regular intervals, representing a stream of cash flow that can be valued today or at a future date. Whether discounted back to the present or compounded forward to the future, an annuity reflects the timevalue relationship between periodic payments and the point in time at which their value is measured.

Capital expenditures (capex): Capital expenditures are funds used to improve or extend the life of the property, such as replacing the roof, making significant renovations, replacing furnaces, and installing air conditioning.

Capitalization rate: This ratio is determined by the net operating income divided by the market value or purchase price. Capitalization rates help value large rental properties and evaluate potential returns. They are used to value income property by dividing the net operating income by a comparable capitalization rate.

Cash flow: The net rental income received after deducting actual operating expenses, financing costs, and regular maintenance expenses but excluding any reserves for infrequent expenses such as capital expenditures.

Cash flow risk: The risk that cash flow needs exceed available cash. If your expenses exceed your income and liquid assets, a lack of cash flow could lead to financial distress or insolvency. This can be mitigated through effective planning.

Cash on cash return: A calculation used to evaluate the profitability of a rental property. It measures the annual return on the money invested by dividing the property's pretax yearly cash flow by the total cash invested.

Currency risk: The potential loss of money resulting from unfavorable fluctuations in currency values. For example, a business that sells products to another country may receive less revenue due to a depreciated currency. Currency risk can be mitigated by employing various strategies such as hedging, diversification, or locking in exchange rates.

Default risk: Default risk applies when any person, company, or government borrows money. Sometimes, borrowers can't make payments due to financial difficulties or other problems. Default risk refers to the likelihood that this will occur. It affects the interest the borrower pays; the higher the default risk, the higher the interest rate.

Depreciation: The gradual decrease in the value of an asset due to wear and tear. In the US, depreciation is a noncash income tax expense that represents the gradual reduction of an asset's recorded cost over its useful life. It's the cost of wear and tear, deterioration, or obsolescence. The IRS allows residential rental properties to be depreciated over 27.5 years. This means you can deduct a portion of the property's cost from your taxable income each year.

Drawdown: This term refers to a drop in price from a peak to the next trough. Drawdown helps assess how difficult it is to maintain an investment or portfolio. When a lender can collect their debt by selling your assets, it is critical because they may force you to sell when prices are temporarily down. For example, an investor who is pyramiding margin on the way up could lose his entire account if the drawdown on the investment exceeds the maintenance margin just after the investor increased their margin to the maximum. Pyramiding involves using leverage to increase a trader's position in the same investment as the price rises. In addition, excessive losses can be challenging to recover from, even without leverage. For example, if you lose 50 percent of your investment, you will need a gain of 100 percent to reach your starting point.

Duration: Duration measures how much your bond's value will change when the interest rate changes. It depends on how long it takes to repay. The longer it takes, the more sensitive your bond's value is to interest rate changes. For example, if you buy a ten-year bond that pays 5 percent interest per year, and the interest rate goes up by 1 percent, your bond's value will drop by about 9 percent. But if you buy a two-year bond that pays 5 percent interest per year, and the interest rate goes up by 1 percent, your bond's value will drop by only about 2 percent.

Fannie Mae: A government-sponsored entity that buys mortgages from lenders, providing them with the funds to offer more loans to borrowers. It packages these purchased loans into mortgage-backed securities (MBS), which are subsequently sold to investors. This process helps to transfer the risk from lenders to investors. Additionally, Fannie Mae focuses on making housing more affordable by increasing mortgage credit availability for low- and moderate-income borrowers.

FDIC: The FDIC insures deposits at member banks up to $250,000 per depositor, per insured bank. The FDIC regulates banks, which also provides some consumer protection.

Freddie Mac: A government-sponsored entity that purchases mortgages from lenders and sells them as MBS. Freddie Mac often collaborates with smaller banks and credit unions, expanding access to mortgage credit across a broader range of financial institutions. By purchasing mortgages and issuing MBS, Freddie Mac helps stabilize and provide liquidity in the mortgage market, particularly during economic downturns.

Gross rent multiplier (GRM): A calculation used to evaluate rental revenue relative to a property's market value. Divide the market value by the annual gross rental income.

Gross rental income: This includes all rental payments received from tenants, as well as any additional income related to the property, such as late fees or pet fees.

Interest rate risk: Interest rate risk refers to the possibility that the value of your bond will decrease if the interest rate increases. This is because when interest rates rise, new bonds will pay more than your bond, making it less attractive to other investors. For example, if you buy a bond that pays 5 percent interest per year, and then the interest rate increases to 6 percent, your bond will be worth less than a new bond that pays 6 percent. If you want to sell your bond, you must sell it at a lower price than you paid.

Internal rate of return (IRR): This rate evaluates profitability. The discount rate makes the net present value (NPV) of all future cash flows equal to zero. IRR is an estimate of yield that considers both rents and resale value. A higher IRR indicates a more profitable investment.

Liquidity risk: When quick sales impact the market price received, temporarily illiquid investments may result in dramatic price swings. For example, imagine you have a rare comic book worth one thousand dollars, but you need five hundred dollars to buy a new phone. You try to sell your comic book online, but no one is interested in buying it right away. You lower the price to eight hundred dollars, but you still have no luck. You are running out of time and want that phone, so you sell your comic book for only four hundred dollars to the first person who makes an offer. You lost six hundred dollars because you had to sell your comic book at a discount. That's liquidity risk. Investments, such as real estate, may be illiquid, presenting both risks and opportunities.

Market maker: A market maker is a broker-dealer who actively quotes both a buy price (bid) and a sell price (ask) for a specific security, continuously standing ready to buy and sell from their own inventory. Their primary function is to provide liquidity and ensure smooth, efficient trading in the financial markets. Market makers may narrow the spread between the bid and ask prices due to competition, thereby lowering transaction costs for investors.

Mortgage-backed securities (MBS): Investment securities that represent a claim on the cash flows from a pool of mortgage loans. Banks sell mortgages to government agencies (such as Fannie Mae/Freddie Mac), which package them into MBS for resale to investors.

Net cash flow: Net operating income minus debt service and reserves for capital expenditures.

Net operating income (NOI): Measures the profitability of income before financing. It is gross rental income minus operating expenses. This does not generally include reserves for capital expenditures.

Net present value (NPV): This is a measure of profitability. It measures the value of an investment by discounting future cash flows back to their present value, accounting for the time value of money at a specified discount rate.

Nominal return: The stated or raw percentage gain on your investment before you account for anything else. Think of it as the headline figure. Nominal return is usually the return in the financial reports.

Operating expenses: The costs incurred to manage and maintain the property. These expenses are necessary to keep the property in good condition and ensure that it remains habitable for tenants. They typically include property management fees, maintenance and repairs, utilities (if paid), property taxes, insurance, advertising and marketing, and attorney or accounting fees. Operating expenses do not include financing costs.

Political risk: Political or regulatory risk can affect investors who buy stocks, bonds, or other assets in a foreign country. For example, imagine you have some money to invest in a country with a fast-growing economy and promising opportunities. You buy some shares of a company that makes solar panels, hoping to profit from the demand for clean energy. But one day, the government of that country decides to increase taxes on foreign investors, impose tariffs on imported goods, or nationalize some industries. These changes make your investment less profitable or even worthless. That's a political risk. There are ways to manage or mitigate political risk. For example, investors can research a country before investing, diversify their investments, or hedge against risk.

Real returns: The actual profits or losses on an investment after accounting for inflation, reflecting the actual increase or decrease in purchasing power. This is distinct from nominal returns, which represent the simple percentage gain without adjusting for external factors.

Risk-free rate: While no investment is truly risk-free, the risk-free rate is the rate with no risk of loss. The risk-free rate serves as a benchmark for assessing bond risk. In practice, the risk-free rate is the interest rate with minimal risk because it is of extremely high quality and short-term. In the US, Treasury bills have historically been used as a proxy for the risk-free rate.

Specific risk: Specific risk refers to the risk of a particular firm or investment, such as business or financial risk. For example, the specific risk of stock investing is choosing the wrong business to invest in. Business risk encompasses competition-related risks. Financial risk encompasses debt, overhead, and cash flow risks. Financial risk can be assessed using financial ratios. Specific risk is a primary concern when investing in individual companies rather than diversified mutual funds. You can reduce specific risks by diversifying. When you invest in particular companies, you should consider a range of qualitative and quantitative risks specific to each company, such as default, liquidity, cash flow, litigation, interest rates, currency, and political risks.

Systematic risk: Systematic or market risk refers to the risk of the entire market or financial system. Systematic risk is macroeconomic risk and may affect multiple asset classes simultaneously. A global recession is an example of systematic risk; many asset classes may move down together during a worldwide recession. You can reduce systematic risk by hedging. Alternatively, you could profit from it by shorting. Investors may pursue lower-risk, liquid, and higher-quality investments during periods of high market risk. So diversifying across some asset classes will protect against systematic risk. Market risk is really just a large number of people expressing a preference for safety over risk. Long-term or strategic asset allocation involves setting target weights for specific asset classes and rebalancing as your portfolio's value changes. This aims to maximize your returns for a given level of volatility.

Vacancy allowance: An allowance for rental income lost due to vacancies. Expressed as a percentage or amount deducted from potential rental income.

FURTHER READING

Mindset

Marcus Aurelius, *Meditations: Adapted for the Contemporary Reader*, trans. James Harris (2016)

James Clear, *Atomic Habits* (2018)

John Paul Getty, *How to Be Rich: His Formulas* (1986)

Napoleon Hill, *Think and Grow Rich* (1937)

Robert T. Kiyosaki, *Rich Dad Poor Dad: What the Rich Teach Their Kids About Money That the Poor and Middle Class Do Not!* (1997)

John C. Maxwell, *The Maxwell Leadership Bible* (2007)

Tony Robbins, *Awaken the Giant Within: How to Take Immediate Control of Your Mental, Emotional, Physical, and Financial Destiny!* (1991)

Tony Robbins, *Unleash the Power Within* (2025)

Sadhguru, *Inner Engineering: A Yogi's Guide to Joy* (2016)

Stephen R. Covey, *The Seven Habits of Highly Effective People* (2003)

Sun-Tzu, *The Art of War*, trans. Ralph D, Sawyer (1994)

For New Investors

David Chilton, *The Wealthy Barber: Everyone's Commonsense Guide to Becoming Financially Independent* (1997)

George Clason, *The Richest Man in Babylon* (2023)

Joel Greenblatt, *The Little Book That Still Beats the Market* (2010)

Robert T. Kiyosaki, *Rich Dad's Cashflow Quadrant: Guide to Financial Freedom* (2010)

Dave Ramsey, *Baby Steps Millionaires* (2022)

Alice Schroeder, *The Snowball: Warren Buffett and the Business of Life* (2008)

Mutual Funds

John C. Bogle, *Bogle on Mutual Funds* (2017)

John C. Bogle, *Common Sense on Mutual Funds* (2012)

Options

Lawrence G. McMillan, *Options as a Strategic Investment, Fourth Edition* (2002)

Real Estate

Michael Boyer, *Every Landlord's Guide to Managing Property: Best Practices from Move-In to Move-Out* (2023)

Mark Ferguson, *Build a Rental Property Empire* (2016)

David M. Greene, *Buy, Rehab, Rent, Refinance, Repeat* (2019)

Craig Hall, *Timing the Real Estate Market* (2004)

Gary Keller, *The Millionaire Real Estate Investor* (2005)

Robert T. Kiyosaki, *The Real Book of Real Estate* (2016)

Brandon Turner, *The Book on Investing in Real Estate with No (and Low) Money Down* (2020)

Brandon Turner and Brandon Murray, *The Multifamily Millionaire, Volume One: Achieve Financial Freedom by Investing in Small Multifamily Real Estate* (2021)

Stocks

Benjamin Graham, *The Intelligent Investor* (1934)

Joel Greenblatt, *You Can Be a Stock Market Genius* (2018)

Peter Lynch, *One Up on Wall Street: How to Use What You Already Know to Make Money in the Market* (2000)

William J. O'Neil, *How to Make Money in Stocks: A Winning System in Good Times or Bad, Fourth Edition* (1988)

Andrew Tobias, *The Only Investment Guide You'll Ever Need* (2022)

Precious Metals and Alternative Productive Assets

Adam Fergusson, *When Money Dies: The Nightmare of Deficit Spending, Devaluation, and Hyperinflation in Weimar Germany* (Weidenfeld & Nicolson, 1975).

David E. Hoffman, *The Oligarchs: Wealth and Power in the New Russia* (Public Affairs, 2002).

Peter Temin, *The Roman Market Economy* (Princeton University Press, 2013).

United States Department of Agriculture, Economic Research Service, "Farm Income and Wealth Statistics," https://ers.usda.gov/data-products/farm-income-and-wealth-statistics, accessed January 2026.

For Further Inspiration

Curtis Faith, *Way of the Turtle: The Secret Methods That Turned Ordinary People into Legendary Traders* (2007)

Max Gunther, *The Very, Very Rich and How They Got That Way: The Spectacular Success Stories of Fifteen Men Who Made It to the Very, Very Top* (2010)

Kaplan/Schweser, *SchweserNotes for the CFA Exam Level I, II, and III* (2009, 2014, 2016)

Reginald F. Lewis and Blair S. Walker, *Why Should White Guys Have All the Fun?* (1995)

Charles Mackay, *Extraordinary Popular Delusions and the Madness of Crowds: All Volumes, Complete and Unabridged* (2016)

Leonard C. MacLean, Edward Thorp, and William Ziemba, eds., *The Kelly Capital Growth Investment Criterion* (2011)

George Soros, *The Alchemy of Finance* (2015)

Rebecca Tapio, Jennifer Eum, and Miguel Morales, eds., *The Forbes 400 Book: Tales of the Richest People in America Since 1982* (2018)

Estate Planning

Alexander A. Bove and Melissa Langa, *The Complete Book of Wills, Estates, and Trusts, Fourth Edition: Advice That Can Save You Thousands of Dollars in Legal Fees and Taxes* (2021)

Ray D. Madoff, *Immortality and the Law: The Rising Power of the American Dead* (2010)

ABOUT EDWARD M. BRADY, CFA, CRCP, REALTOR

Edward M. Brady strives for excellence in body, mind, and spirit, pursuing living life to the fullest. To retire freely and with integrity, love, health, travel, and experiences requires a disciplined approach to personal finance.

With over twenty-five years of experience conducting compliance examinations, Edward built a reputation for integrity and diligence. At the SEC, he was known for his tenacity, technical acumen, and sharp analytical mind. Edward has conducted hundreds of examinations of broker-dealers, FINRA, transfer agents, and investment advisors to ensure adherence to federal securities laws.

His work did not stop with analysis. Edward authored influential reports and letters, trained new examiners, and even became a sought-after speaker at industry and military outreach events.

During his career, Edward served in the army reserve for ten years; while in the service, he took up natural bodybuilding as a hobby.

Edward has received numerous awards from the SEC, the US Army, and in bodybuilding. His career reflects his commitment to excellence and public service.

Academically, Edward graduated cum laude from California State University, Northridge, with a degree in finance. He passed exams for several professional credentials, including CFA, certified fraud examiner, certified regulatory compliance professional, and the CFA Institute's Data Science for Investment Professionals certificate.

Today, Edward is a writer, agent, and investor. As a Realtor, his focus is to serve clients' goals by simplifying complex transactions and making them smoother and less stressful. As a licensed California real estate broker (DRE#01066142), Edward offers brokerage services through eXp Realty, Inc. (DRE#02187306). As an investor, Edward practices a disciplined approach to preserve personal freedom.

Residing in California with his family, Edward balances professional excellence with personal fulfillment, pursuing fitness, finances, learning, service, and spiritual growth through regular prayer and meditation.

www.ingramcontent.com/pod-product-compliance
Lightning Source LLC
LaVergne TN
LVHW090403210926
848480LV00002B/432